Anchorage

CITY HISTORY SERIES

Anchorage
Fairbanks

CITY HISTORY SERIES

Anchorage

FROM ITS HUMBLE ORIGINS AS A RAILROAD CONSTRUCTION CAMP

E·L·I·Z·A·B·E·T·H   T·O·W·E·R

EPICENTER PRESS

FAIRBANKS · SEATTLE

Epicenter Press, Inc., is a regional press founded in Alaska whose interests include but are not limited to the arts, history, environment, and diverse cultures and lifestyles of the North Pacific and high latitudes. We seek both the traditional and innovative in publishing high-quality nonfiction tradebooks, contemporary art and photography giftbooks, and destination travel guides emphasizing Alaska, Washington, Oregon, and California.

Cover Photo: Front—After Congress approved Statehood for Alaska, Rita Martin, the future wife of U.S. Sen. Mike Gravel, attached a 49th star to a giant U.S. flag draped over the side of the old Federal Building in downtown Anchorage; Back (top)—Anchorage began as a tent city at the mouth of Ship Creek, which in 1915 was designated a construction camp for a new federal railroad; Back (middle)—Downtown Anchorage was heavily damaged in the 1964 Earthquake; Back (bottom)—The historic Fourth Avenue Theater remains an icon of downtown Anchorage. Photos from the Anchorage Museum of History & Art

Editor: J. Stephen Lay
Cover and inside design: Elizabeth Watson
Proofreader: Lois Kelly
Maps: L. W. Nelson
Printer: Transcontinental Printing, Inc.
Text © 1999 by Elizabeth Tower

Library of Congress Catalog Card Number: 99-072501

Printed in CANADA
First printing, April 1999
10 9 8 7 6 5 4 3 2 1

To order single copies of this title, mail $14.95 (WA residents add $1.29 state sales tax) plus $5 for priority-mail shipping to: Epicenter Press, Box 82368, Kenmore, WA 98028-0368. Booksellers: Retail discounts are available from our trade distributor, Graphic Arts Center Publishing Co. Box 10306, Portland, OR 97210. Phone 800-452-3032

To my children
Chris, Steve and Alice
and others who, like them , grew up in Anchorage
and stayed to make this city
home for their families.

Table of Contents

Girdwood, a small mining town to the south of Anchorage, was the largest settlement in the region before the establishment of the railroad construction site at Ship Creek.

Foreword

In 1970, while mayor of Anchorage, I traveled to Norway to visit our sister city of Tromso. Enroute, we stopped in Bergen, where I called on the vice-lord mayor, who informed me that Bergen was celebrating its 800th birthday. In Anchorage, we were celebrating our city's 50th!

Our history is so recent. And for that reason it can be an intensely personal thing, too. Many of the city's early settlers and their sons and daughters are still with us today and still living in Anchorage. I could not help but reflect on my own family's story as I read Elizabeth Tower's absorbing, entertaining, and meticulously researched history of Anchorage.

My maternal grandfather, Hugh Murray, came north in the early 1890s and operated a fish cannery in Southeast Alaska before moving to Valdez shortly after the turn of the century. He owned and operated a steamship carrying passenger and freight throughout Prince William Sound, where he also was active in copper mining.

My father, Harvey Sullivan, and four of his brothers were drawn by the Klondike gold discovery. They arrived in Skagway in February 1898, just in time to help rescue climbers buried in an avalanche that claimed many lives on the Dyea Trail. They mined in the Dawson area, then moved on to Nome. In 1907, Dad made his way to Valdez, where he met my mother. They were married in 1912 and raised my two sisters and me.

Our first visit to Anchorage was in the early 1930s. We stayed at the Anchorage Hotel, and I still recall vividly the thrill of flying with Frank Dorbrant in a Tri-Motor Ford airplane. I returned in 1937 and 1939 when Valdez High School played in the annual Anchorage Fur Rendezvous basketball tournament. After living in Nenana and Fairbanks for several years, I returned to Anchorage in 1958, the year Congress approved Statehood for Alaska, and

Anchorage is where Margaret and I reside today, along with eight of our nine grown children.

Anchorage is a dynamic, fast-changing place, as are so many young cities in developing regions, and its history is closely inter-twined with the development of modern Alaska both influencing and influenced by national and global events.

Elizabeth Tower captures all of this—the recent, the personal, the ever-changing and far-reaching, and certainly the dynamic history of Alaska's largest city.

George M. Sullivan
Mayor of Anchorage, 1967-1982

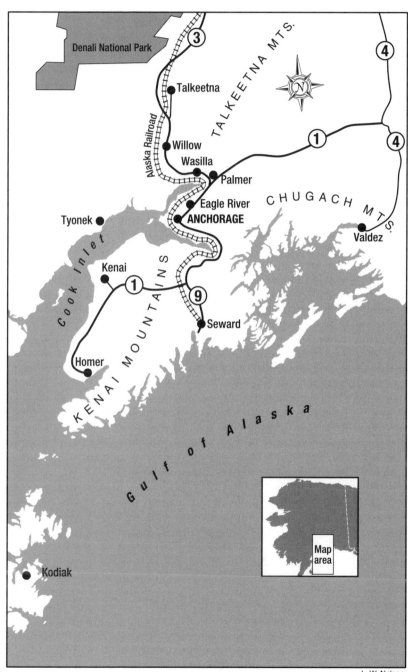

L. W. Nelson

11

1

Arrival of White Settlers

Ship Creek, in 1912, gave no indication that it would grow into Alaska's largest city and the home to more than a quarter of a million people in less then eight decades.

Shem Pete, a fourteen-year-old Dena'ina Indian boy, witnessed the birth of Anchorage in 1915 when he came from Susitna Station in a dory to sell his bear skins. He didn't see any buildings, but there were lots of tents housing opportunists who flocked to the banks of Ship Creek upon hearing a major construction camp would be located there. President Woodrow Wilson had selected the western route up the Susitna River valley for the new government railroad to Fairbanks.

13

Shem joined the rush for a while and watched white newcomers working. "They burn and cut the trees," he recalled years later. "It's full of smoke, fire, night time. They like to work the night time too. It's too hot day time, June month, so a lot of people working. And I work in the restaurant. For about two weeks. And they play cards. Lots of gambling in the tent."

Shem returned to his village at Susitna to go to school, but his life had changed forever. "There used to be a lot of people at Susitna, at least 600 or 700 Natives. And whooping cough, that one came along and killed quite a few. And then measles come....Then the third time, 1918, the flu come....I lose my mother the first day....It pretty near cleaned up all the Susitna people....Gee whiz, we got pretty lonesome. We're only a few people left." Shem Pete was one of three young men who dug most of the graves at Susitna in the winter of 1918-1919.

The Dena'ina (Tanaina) Indians lived a subsistence life in the upper Cook Inlet area of Southcentral Alaska without much interference from white settlers prior to the railroad construction. These Indians, the only Athabaskans living in a coastal region, entered Cook Inlet through mountain passes to the west as early as 500 A.D. displacing Alutiiq Eskimos, from whom they adapted coastal technology, such as the use of kayaks for salt water fishing. Traditional Dena'ina stories tell of battles at Point Campbell and Green Lake with Eskimos who came over Portage Pass from Prince William Sound or up Cook Inlet from Kodiak Island. Recent linguistic research indicates that the Natives who met Captain Cook in kayaks when he entered Cook Inlet in 1778 may have been Dena'ina Athabaskans rather than Eskimos.

Indians migrated with the seasons. In the summer they fished on inlet streams and hunted beluga whale from their kayaks. Shem Pete noted that the mouth of Ship Creek was a particularly productive salmon fishing site, which they could count on to prevent starvation. They built shelters along the upper reaches of Ship Creek, Peters Creek, and Eklutna Lake to use when hunting mountain sheep and goats. In the fall they found caribou in the foothills surrounding upper Cook Inlet and moose and beaver in the swampy muskeg of the Anchorage bowl. Their winter villages were generally located at junctions of trading routes. The upper inlet Dena'ina carried on active trading with the Ahtna Indians of the Copper River at villages along upper Knik Arm and with the lower inlet Dena'ina at Point McKenzie across Cook Inlet from the mouth of Ship Creek. Although Russian fur traders established permanent posts along the shores of lower Cook Inlet, the upper inlet Dena'ina successfully resisted encroachment. The only Russian presence in the upper inlet was a winter trading post at Niteh on the delta between the Matanuska and Knik Rivers, established in 1844 with a small agricultural settlement nearby. Malakhov ascended the Susitna River in 1834 or 1844, but the Russians made little attempt to map the area. The Dena'ina adopted some Russian words and names and welcomed Orthodox missionaries, who established a mission at Knik on the western shore of Knik Arm around 1835. However, the Russians brought smallpox and tuberculosis along with their language and religion. The Dena'ina population of the upper inlet in 1845 was estimated at only 816, about half the number that Russians had counted a decade earlier.

After the United States purchased Russian America in 1867, white prospectors started entering the region to look for gold by ascending the Susitna River or by crossing Portage Pass from Prince William Sound to Turnagain Arm. Large vessels usually stopped at Tyonek, where prospectors transferred to smaller boats in order to enter Knik and Turnagain Arms on the high tide. The Alaska Commercial Company, which took over the assets of the Russian American Company, opened stores at Tyonek about 1875, at Knik in 1882, and at Susitna Station shortly thereafter. The Dena'ina trapped and traded furs with the store owners and with cannery ships that began entering Cook Inlet to fish. By the end of the 19th century, commercial activity with its associated temptations had become so pervasive at Knik that the Indians dismantled their Orthodox mission and moved it to Eklutna (Ikluat), the site of an old Dena'ina village on the east side of upper Knik Arm.

The most successful gold mining in the Cook Inlet region prior to 1900 was near Sunrise City and Hope on the south shore and at Girdwood on the north shore of Turnagain Arm. In 1895, gold mining began in this Turnagain district, which was one of the most active mining districts in Alaska until many miners left for the Yukon in 1897. They heard

Girdwood was the site of a successful gold-mining operation in 1900.

about the Klondike strike from Captain Austin E. Lathrop, who transported prospectors and supplies from Tyonek to Sunrise City and Hope in his sailing schooner, *L.J. Perry.*

Most prospectors heading for the Yukon or the Alaskan gold fields at Circle City and Rampart either crossed through Canada on trails from Skagway or took the long water route up the Yukon River from St. Michael. The United States government answered demands for an all-American overland route to the gold fields in 1898 by sending Army exploring expeditions to Alaska to study possible routes. One expedition, under Captain William Abercrombie, started at Valdez, where several thousand stampeders were already ascending Valdez Glacier to the headwaters of the Klutina River, a tributary of the Copper. A second Army expedition, commanded by Captain Edward Glenn, had orders to look for a glacier-free trail from Portage Bay on Prince William Sound to Turnagain Arm and to study routes up the Matanuska and Susitna Rivers to interior Alaska. Glenn divided his troops in 1898 and 1899 into several smaller parties, one of which ascended the Matanuska River to reach the Copper River country through Tahneta Pass, the current route of the Glenn Highway. Another group went up the Susitna River and through Broad Pass to the Nenana River, and still another passed through the Alaska mountain range to the south fork of the Kuskokwim River. A party that included the geologist Walter Mendenhall pioneered the trail through Crow Pass from Turnagain Arm to Eagle River that was used several years later to reach the gold fields in the Iditarod district.

In his report, Glenn recommended a site at the mouth of the Susitna River and one "at or near Palmer's cache, which is the head of navigation, and where good anchorage can be obtained for seagoing vessels" as potential locations for military bases. Palmer's store was located at Knik and the anchorage mentioned was probably in deep water north of Fire

Anchorage Museum of History and Art

Two early explorers were U.S. Army Captain Edward Glenn, left, and Walter Mendenhall.

Island. Glenn apparently overlooked the flat area around the mouths of Ship Creek and Eagle River where Anchorage and the military bases are now located. He concluded that there was "no doubt that a railroad could be readily constructed from Tyoonok [sic] up the Sushitna [sic] River Valley and thence via the trail followed by the Van Schoonhoven party to the Tanana" but that "there is as yet practically no development either of agricultural or mineral resources of the Cook Inlet or country tributary to it that warrants even the contemplation of a railroad therein."

Captain Glenn's conclusion that a railroad in the Cook Inlet area was not justified did not deter one eager railroad builder: Major John E. Ballaine, who had been a secretary to the governor of Washington. He returned from the Spanish-American War with the conviction that he could open the Alaska interior with a railroad along an all-American route. Since he needed a deep-water port for his railroad and a town site that could accommodate 500,000 people, he studied information about Tyonek, Knik, Port Wells, Valdez, Cordova Bay, Controller Bay, and Resurrection Bay. He decided that only Resurrection Bay would satisfy his requirements and sold stock in his railroad enterprise throughout the United States and Canada.

In 1902, eight survey crews, consisting of seventy-six men under Chief Engineer Charles M. Anderson, conducted a preliminary survey from Resurrection Bay to the Tanana River. Their original right-of-way bypassed the current site of downtown Anchorage by turning north at Potter and skirting the mountains to cross Eagle River well inland from Knik Arm.

In 1903, the Tanana Construction Company started building the Alaska Central Railroad from Ballaine's new town of Seward. The contractors had laid fifty miles of track by the end of 1905, but railroad construction in Alaska proved to be more expensive than Ballaine predicted. He had already spent almost two million dollars, and there was no government aid forthcoming. Railroad builders had previously enjoyed low-rate loans and federal subsidies, but by the time railroad development in Alaska was being considered, the government was more anxious to prevent railroad monopolies than to stimulate development. Rather than receiving subsidies, developers in

Alaska were restricted in the amount of time allowed for completion of the railroad. Furthermore, they were taxed $100 by the federal government for each mile of operating track whether or not the railroad was making a profit. Unable to get adequate private financing, the Alaska Central Railroad declared bankruptcy and went into receivership. After a complete reorganization, the promoters reappeared as the Alaska Northern Railroad and constructed an additional twenty-two miles of track to Kern Creek on Turnagain Arm. They finally gave up the effort in 1909 and abandoned the tracks.

On Prince William Sound, railroad promoters attracted enough private capital to build a successful standard gauge railroad because they had an asset the Cook Inlet promoters lacked—a potentially profitable copper discovery in the Wrangell Mountains that required a railroad to bring ore to tidewater. After several abortive efforts to build a railroad from the port of Valdez had culminated in warfare at Keystone Canyon between rival railroad builders, the Copper River and Northwestern Railroad, financed by the Morgan-Guggenheim Alaska Syndicate, completed 196 miles of track from Cordova to the Kennecott Copper Mine in 1911. The fatal shooting at Keystone Canyon added to the unpopularity of the Alaska Syndicate, which some Alaskans accused of attempting to monopolize Alaska's mineral and commercial assets.

The Alaskan railroad situation achieved national notoriety in 1910 during the Pinchot-Ballinger hearings in Washington, D.C. In an attempt to discredit development-minded Secretary of Interior Richard Ballinger, Chief Forester Gifford Pinchot, an avowed conservationist, accused Ballinger of trying to help the Alaska Syndicate acquire coal claims in the Bering River coal fields southeast of Cordova.

James Wickersham, Alaska's delegate to Congress, entered the debate for political reasons of his own and helped to rally antimonopoly forces in opposition to the Alaska Syndicate. The financial backers of the Copper River and Northwestern Railroad announced that they would suspend plans to set tracks beyond Chitina to the Yukon River unless the federal government opened Alaska coal lands, which the government had closed to entry in 1906.

Access to coal was an important reason for considering railroad development in Alaska because Navy vessels still burned coal and the United States did not have domestic coal sources on the West Coast. The major potential Alaska coal fields were the Bering River coal fields, which could be reached by a spur from the Copper River and Northwestern, and the Matanuska coal fields that might be reached by a railroad in the Cook Inlet area. The publicity surrounding the Pinchot-Ballinger controversy made it unlikely that any private railroad would provide access to coal in Alaska. If the United States Navy needed Alaskan coal, the federal government would have to build the railroad itself. In 1912 Delegate Wickersham succeeded in getting Congress to pass legislation enabling the building of a government railroad in Alaska along a route to be determined by the president. Both the Alaska Northern Railroad and the Copper River and Northwestern Railroad were offered for sale, with the functioning Copper River line commanding a considerably higher price than the defunct Alaska Northern.

The initial recommendation to President William Howard Taft was that both railroads should be purchased, with the Copper River and Northwestern extended to Fairbanks and the Alaska Northern extended both to the Matanuska coal fields and to the Kuskokwim Valley. By the time a final decision on railroad routes had to be made, Democrat Woodrow Wilson was president. Wilson was reluctant to endorse the recommendations of his Republican predecessor, whose administration had taken such a beating during the Pinchot-Ballinger debate. Wilson appointed three men, William C. Edes, Thomas Riggs, and Lt. Frederick Mears, to the Alaska Engineering Commission and instructed them to make further study of potential railroad routes. Edes and Mears recognized the assets of the Ship Creek site because it provided easy access to the Matanuska coal fields, adequate area for development of a large construction camp, coal bunkers, and railroad yards, and a port that, in spite of ice floes during the winter, could be used at least six months of the year. President Wilson was relieved to have justification for avoiding purchase of the Copper River and Northwestern Railroad from the unpopular Morgan-Guggenheim Syndicate, even though the Copper River route, which served an active mining region, would have been more profitable for the government. Thus the scene was set for the creation of Anchorage, which would become the transportation hub of Alaska. ∎

Colonel James Girdwood

James Girdwood, the twenty-year-old son of a Dublin linen merchant, arrived in New York City in 1862 with $400 in his pocket. He went to work as a linen salesman. By age thirty-four he controlled over half of the Irish linen market in the United States. When he sold out in 1894, he pledged never to return to the linen business; he prospected for gold in Alaska instead. Although most stampeders who came to Turnagain Arm in 1896 settled at Hope and Sunrise City, Girdwood built his cabin at Glacier City, a small distribution settlement on the north side of the Arm.

In 1900 Girdwood staked four claims on Crow Creek and formed the Crow Creek Alaska Hydraulic Gold Mining Co. His mining venture was so successful that, in subsequent years, his bullion income exceeded $106,000 a year. Furthermore, he was so popular with fellow miners that they accorded him the honorary title of "colonel" and renamed the town for him.

While developing the Crow Creek gold mines, Girdwood staked copper claims on Latouche Island. On January 4, 1907, the Latouche Copper Mining Company was formed in New York with James Girdwood as president and his Turnagain Arm gold-mining property as a subsidiary. Between 1900 and 1910, Girdwood became a close friend of Daniel and Isaac Guggenheim, and he subsequently sold the Latouche copper claims to the Kennecott Copper Company.

Girdwood retained his gold mining claims on Turnagain Arm and, in 1923, bought several lots in the town of Girdwood. (In the early 1980s these lots were still owned by his grandson.) Although he stopped active mining for a while because of restrictions on hydraulic mining, James Girdwood planned to reopen the mine in 1926. He made major investments in flumes and machinery until ill health cut short his plans. He died at his West Orange, New Jersey, estate in March 1928. ∎

The Last Dena'ina Chief

Mike Alex was born at Eklutna village near the turn of the century. He came from the Cheesi, Clan of the Color Red, and from the Nulchina, Clan of the Sky People. His father, Alex Vasily, nicknamed Eklutna Alex by railroaders, was born at "Hutnaynut'i," a large Dena'ina village in the Bodenburg Butte area near Palmer. His mother, Matrona, was from Susitna village. Both Alex and his brother, Theodore Vasily (Chief Wassila), were Dena'ina shamans. Alex was also a devout Orthodox Christian, who traveled nearly 200 miles in midwinter by sled to have his six-month-old son Mike baptized on February 29, 1908, in the Russian Orthodox church at Kenai.

As a child Mike migrated throughout the upper Cook Inlet area with his family, spending summers at a large fish camp on the banks of Ship Creek and winters in Eklutna village, where he could watch miners mushing over the trail to Iditarod and surrounding gold camps. In 1915 railroad construction forced the Indians to move from their Ship Creek fish camp and smokehouse, located where the Elevation 29 Restaurant now stands, to camps on Fire Island. Eklutna Alex had hunting cabins at both ends of Eklutna Lake.

Mike could not attend classes at the Eklutna Industrial School, established in 1924 by the United States Department of Education for Native children orphaned in the influenza epidemic; he had to help support the family of thirteen children. Mike regretted his lack of education—particularly not knowing enough Russian to qualify for the Orthodox clergy. He married Daria Nellie, the daughter of Ephim (Beqenugeydghety Tukdu), the chief of the Susitna Dena'ina. Ephim, who was a shaman, predicted the death of his tribe in the 1919 flu epidemic and sent Daria and her brother away from Susitna so they could survive. Mike worked for the Alaska Railroad for almost thirty years and was a section foreman from 1944 to 1957, when heart trouble forced him to retire. In the summers he fished at Fire Island and instructed Eklutna School students in setting nets near the mouth of Eagle River. The Eklutna School closed after World War II. When Eklutna Alex died in 1953, he instructed Mike, his eldest son, to take over as caretaker

Anchorage Museum of History and Art

The St. Nicholas Orthodox Church (circa 1955) served Eklutna for many years.

of the St. Nicholas Orthodox Church and Cemetery at Eklutna. Shortly after his father's death, Mike was hospitalized for six months with heart trouble. He attributed his recovery to Orthodox Metropolitan Leonty from New York, who gave him confession and blessed him during a visit to Eklutna. Subsequently, Mike helped raise money to build St. Innocent Church in Anchorage. During the United States Bicentennial, Eklutna village secured two grants for reconstruction of St. Nicholas Church. Work began on September 23, 1976, under the direction of Mike and his son Daniel. Mike died in 1977 after completing the reconstruction and building a new church with money raised by selling postcards and slides of the old church and cemetery.

Several times the U.S. government tried to eliminate Eklutna village and turn the land over to other people, but Mike Alex, as village chief, hired lawyers, first William Paul and later Stanley McCutcheon, with his own money to stop the government. The Alaska Native Claims Settlement Act of 1971 now protects Eklutna village, and a corporate board has responsibilities formerly held by a tribal chief. Eklutna, Inc., formed a year after passage of ANCSA, filed claims in August 1973 for part of Chugach State Park around Eklutna Lake and for the land where Chugiak High School and Birchwood Elementary School are located. In January 1978, Daniel Alex, as spokesman for Eklutna, Inc., gave legal consent for the Anchorage School District to continue undisputed use of this land in perpetuity. Dan Alex, who graduated from Alaska Methodist University (now Alaska Pacific University) in 1964, was the first member of his family to receive a college degree. After the passage of ANCSA, he returned from Washington, D.C., where he was a Navy geophysicist, to take over management of Eklutna, Inc.

In the ensuing years, Eklutna, Inc. has suffered from instability, but, in 1998, Dan Alex is again president of the five-member board of directors, which has hired a professional manager and renegotiated loans. Eklutna, Inc. owns 70,000 acres of land between Eagle River and Eklutna village, which is not taxed until it is developed. Only twenty-six acres of land is to be developed each year to prevent flooding the market. Eklutna Lake will continue to be managed as a state park and, according to the 1982 North Anchorage Land Agreement, 17,500 acres will revert to Eklutna, Inc. if and when Fort Richardson is closed. Fifty people currently live in Eklutna village. St. Nicholas Church, the Mike Alex cabin, and the Orthodox cemetery where Mike is buried are now part of the Eklutna Historical Park The 143 stockholders of Eklutna, Inc., descendants of the Dena'ina Indians who were driven from their Ship Creek fish camps by railroad builders in 1915, are potentially the largest land holders in the Anchorage bowl. ■

2

Town Site Auction

The first railroad track in Anchorage ran right through the temporary tent city housing its workers into the "commercial district" with the Montana Pool Hall in the background.

Southcentral Alaska nervously awaited the official announcement of the route for the new government railroad during the spring of 1915. Seward was optimistic about a resurrection of the defunct Alaska Northern Railway, while Cordova hoped their Washington, D.C. lobbyist, George C. Hazelet, could successfully point out the economic advantages of acquiring the functioning Copper River and Northwestern Railroad. Even Valdez experienced a railroad fever revival. However, the major activity took place on Cook Inlet across Knik Arm from Knik, the boom town that served as supply depot for prospectors heading to Iditarod and other mining camps in the Kuskokwim Valley.

Sourdoughs from all Alaska, as well as businessmen from the Pacific Northwest, flocked to Ship Creek's banks, where the federal government had reserved land for a potential town site, along with land in several other areas such as Nenana and Chitna that might be along the chosen railroad route. Many of these optimists had followed the gold rushes from the Klondike and Circle City to Nome and Fairbanks and then Iditarod and Ruby, but activity in the gold fields was slowing down. The 1913-1914 flurry of prospecting activity at remote Chisana near the Canadian border had been disappointing. Railroad construction offered the best hope for employment, and commercial developers anticipated that "mining" the railroad workers would be their most lucrative option.

The area around the mouth of Ship Creek, where vessels could anchor in deep water awaiting high tide to lighter supplies to shore, was relatively undeveloped when the Alaska Engineering Commission had studied it in the summer of 1914. Michael Carberry and Donna Lane, who inventoried Anchorage's historic resources in *Patterns of the Past*, found the J.D. Whitneys had a homestead cabin about four miles up Ship Creek; Chugach National Forest employees Keith McCullough and Jack Brown had cabins in the area, as did a squatter named Thomas Jeter. G.W. Palmer, who started the Knik trading post around the turn of the century, had a warehouse along the shoreline, about three miles north of Ship Creek. They made no mention of the Dena'ina Indian fishing sites and smokehouses. Ship Creek became the field headquarters of the Commission in 1914 and a few log buildings were constructed for the staff. Anticipating President Wilson's favorable reaction to their report, the Commission left a small crew behind to build a mess hall and hospital during the winter.

While awaiting official word that Ship Creek would be the site of a railroad construction camp, new squatters started arriving in March and settled on the north bank of the creek, under the high ground now known as Government Hill. To get a head start on their commercial endeavors,

Anchorage Museum of History and Art

When building the "first" Anchorage along the water, merchants knew their stay would be short and they built ready to move. The buildings in the photo of the old town are all on temporary foundations so they could be easily moved when the time came.

many erected wall tents and buildings on skids so they could eventually be moved to permanent locations in the new town. They were encouraged when President Wilson made the expected announcement on April 9, 1915, and Commissioner Frederick Mears arrived on April 26 to take charge.

The Alaska Engineering Commission divided the railroad route into three sections. Chairman William Edes, a fifty-eight-year-old graduate of Massachusetts Institute of Technology with years of railroad engineering experience, would spend equal time at the A.E.C. headquarters in Seward and in Washington, D.C. Thomas Riggs, a surveyor who had worked on the Alaska Boundary Survey and would later be appointed governor of Alaska, had his headquarters in Fairbanks with responsibility for the segment of railroad between Fairbanks and Broad Pass. Lieutenant Frederick Mears, youngest of the commissioners, was responsible for 230 miles of railroad construction between the head of Turnagain Arm and Broad Pass in addition to the tracks to the Matanuska coal fields.

Mears was well-qualified for his work on the Alaska Railroad. He started his railroad career at age nineteen as a chainman on the Great Northern Railroad. In 1898, he was promoted to assistant engineer and worked on locating the Kootenai Valley and the Bellingham & Neson Railroads in northern Idaho and British Columbia. In 1899, Mears enlisted in the United States Army and was sent to the Philippines during the Spanish-American War. He was commissioned as a Second Lieutenant in 1901 and was assigned to the United Staff College at Fort Leavenworth, Kansas, upon his return to the United States. In May 1906, he was sent to Panama at the request of John F. Stevens, chief engineer on the Panama Canal, with whom he had worked on the Great Northern Railroad. In 1909 Lieut. Mears became chief engineer of the Panama Railroad. Work under his supervision in Panama included: reconstruction of almost the entire railway; design and construction of the Atlantic terminal docks at Colon; location survey for the Panama government of a railway from the Canal Zone to the Costa Rican border; and construction of numerous structures for the Panama Railroad, amounting to over $11 million. Work on the Panama Canal and railroad was drawing to a close, so Mears brought with him government supplies that had been used in Panama, including dredging equipment to improve the harbor at Ship Creek.

Mears was soon aware that serious problems were developing in the tent city on the flats at Ship Creek. There were no sewers and Cook Inlet tides provided the only means of waste disposal. In May the Commission surgeon warned that the water supply would become contaminated if settlement on the flats continued much longer. Mears also wanted regulations to prohibit liquor traffic in the new town site. Andrew Christensen, the Land Office chief of field division in charge of the surveys, arrived from Juneau on May 24 and quickly completed surveying a 350-acre site on higher ground south of Ship Creek. The Anchorage plan was typical of railroad town planning in the western states and territories. All roads and lots were at right angles—the only exception being Christensen Road, appropriately named for Andrew—which ascended a bluff too steep for a T-square road. East-west streets were named numerically and north-south streets alphabetically. According to one Land Office commissioner, the only excuse for such lack of imagination was that the town was urgently needed and was hurriedly laid out by engineers whose primary purpose was to build a railroad.

Although the regularity of the plan and the scarcity of amenities such as parks brought criticism from the National Municipal League, the

Anchorage Museum of History and Art

The only way to keep dry feet and avoid getting stuck in the mud was to stay on this boardwalk crossing the mud flats to the Ship Creek landing.

Land Office survey was approved and July 10 was selected to auction the lots. On June 19, President Wilson issued detailed rules—no lot could be sold for less than $25 with the purchaser to pay in full or one-third down and the balance in five equal installments. Regulations further stipulated that the lots and the payments made for them would be forfeited if the property was "used for the purpose of manufacturing, selling, or otherwise disposing of intoxicating liquors as a beverage, or for gambling, prostitution, or any unlawful purpose..." A reserve district was set aside beyond the town site boundaries for prostitution because the government recognized that control would be easier outside of town than within the town, where forfeiture of lots would be required.

Christensen served as auctioneer on July 10. Bidding was so brisk that prospective owners were unable to hold down prices. When sales closed a week later, 655 lots had been sold for almost $150,000. A few successful bidders acquired as many as ten lots, paying up to $4,000, but the speculation that many feared did not occur, and Christensen claimed the sale had "injected confidence in the people of the town."

A few weeks later, the A.E.C. issued an order requiring all tents be moved from the Ship Creek flats to the new town site no later than August 16th. The order to evacuate the flats was a bonanza for people lucky enough to own a wagon and a team of horses. Some lot owners promptly moved their tents or buildings; others erected new frame buildings on their lots. On August 14, the *Cook Inlet Pioneer and Knik News*, which had moved from Knik and now occupied a building on Block 43, Lot 7, announced "FINE BUILDINGS ADORN NEW TOWN" and that "Captain Austin Lathrop enjoys the distinction of erecting the most commodious building in town" located at the corner of Fourth Avenue and H Street. Lathrop, who had transported prospectors down Turnagain Arm to Hope and Sunrise in his sailing schooner during the 1895-97 gold rush, had already erected a similar building and a movie theater in Cordova and planned to do the same in Anchorage.

Although the new town site had often been referred to as "Knik Anchorage" and then just "Anchorage," some residents had other choices for a name. To settle the matter, an election was held on August 9, 1915.

Anchorage Museum of History and Art

The sound of building echoed throughout Anchorage during the summer of 1915. Every one of these buildings along 4th Avenue was under construction.

Anchorage Museum of History and Art

The Yukon Rooms, a tent boarding house, was placed on skids and moved up the hill to 4th Avenue when the town moved from the flats below the city.

Anchorage won by a considerable majority over the other names on the ballot, which included Matanuska, Alaska City, Ship Creek, Winalaska, Gateway, Terminal, Homestead, and Lane.

The Land Office continued to sell lots and lease business sites in the terminal area. After two successful sales during November, Christensen expressed the opinion that he could sell lots in Anchorage every day because demand never ceased. ■

Anchorage—1916

As seen by a *Wandering Boy*

Kenneth Gideon, a University of Washington engineering student who lived in Alaska between 1913 and 1918, recorded his impressions of the territory in *Wandering Boy*. While working at the Crow Creek Mine in Girdwood during the 1915 summer, he and his friends considered going to Anchorage and bidding on some land, but they got "cold feet" and didn't appear in Anchorage until late fall when work at the mine stopped. That first fall he stayed at the Crist House, run by George Crist, an old-time Seattle streetcar man, where he paid fifty cents a night for one of twenty or thirty cots in the attic.

Soon Gideon and a friend from the mine "went in together on a couple of buildings, one housed a hardware store and the other housed us and a business venture of the first water—a hand-laundry." Gideon described the laundry operation. "One day Dan ran across a fellow with a laundry and he talked me into making a deal whereby the three of us would operate this trap. In that way we would have something to do that winter. That was the way we figured and that was the way it worked out—we had something to do. In fact, I never had so much to do in all my life, nor do I ever expect to again.

"The water mains weren't in yet and you can't run a laundry without water, so I got a sled and two fifty-gallon barrels. Down at the end of the street was a spring that supplied the entire neighborhood. I had to drag those two barrels full of water over from the spring, and when that part was taken care of, I pounded clothes in the tub. I didn't like it and Dan didn't like it, so we finally bought our third partner out and went out of the laundry business."

Gideon blamed his problems on the town administration: "The usual government bungling was to be seen in about everything that was done. They didn't start to lay the water mains till the freezing weather started and the frozen earth was dumped in the trenches on top of the mains. They all froze solid and all that winter they were driving steam into them trying to get them open. Probably the local officials were capable enough, but someone in a position of authority the length and breadth of a continent away insisted in displaying his authority by refusing to be hurried and as a result Anchorage hauled water on sleds."

Immigrants were discriminated against in early Anchorage, according to Gideon. "In those first few months a great crowd of central Europeans poured into Anchorage causing a race problem. They came mostly from the recently completed Grand Trunk Railroad and the Americans found it difficult to compete with them. The government had set a very low scale of wages—low, at least, for Alaska—and what with the uncertainty of appropriations and a surplus of those boys, the prospect for a boom town looked dark. A block or so was set off to one side for them and they built themselves hovels and shelters—dog kennels would be a better name. Half a dozen of them would hole up in one little box with shelf-like bunks along the wall. In this way one stove would suffice; in fact, the one I saw would have been better off without a stove. A sardine would have choked. Uptown one pool hall was given over to their exclusive use and they were discouraged from visiting any other."

Gideon also observed government efforts to keep Anchorage a dry town. "The government had decreed that there was to be no liquor sold in Anchorage nor in a five-mile strip on either side of the railroad right-of-way. The effect was to make bootlegging a science in Anchorage. In the winter liquor came in over the trail, on hand sleds and by dog team. In the summer when navigation opened up it might be found in five-gallon cans inside bales of hay. Cases of canned tomatoes would prove other than tomatoes. A goodly percentage of it found its way down to the Line and, once there, it enjoyed immunity from search and seizure, for the law stayed away from The Line. If some miner just in from the hills went down there and lost his roll, that was sad indeed. Tsk, tsk. People should stay away from such places. If he socked the girl on the jaw and got it back, that was one on the girl."

In spite of his admonitions to the contrary, Gideon eventually visited The Line. "In our crowd that came in from the mine that fall were several young fellows my age and some oldsters with young

Anchorage Museum of History and Art

The Hotel Crist where the "wandering boy" lived part of the time when in Anchorage.

ideas. These latter ones had gullets lined with zinc and that bootleg whiskey only warmed them up. We prowled around the place for awhile and it was inevitable that sooner or later someone would suggest we take in the red lights. O.K., we'd go. I knew what to expect, having heard about these fancy joints that looked so good— all plush carpets, divans with leopard skin rugs, silk curtains, and rose petals, with a big turbaned Senegambian serving wine....

"There was quite a gap between the main town and the block of houses where these women were, but a person could have found the place in a London fog. There must have been fifteen or twenty phonographs going at once, old-time phonographs of the scratch and screech variety, and the evening air was shuddering under the impact of sound. We started down the walk and as we did so, a female longshoreman with her hair over one ear leaned out of the upper half of a door and, in the mellow tone of a diesel truck, said 'Hyah, boys, come in and get warm.'

"We went in. One of the old-timers said he'd buy a drink, and the dreadful apparition went out in the back room. I looked around. No rose petals. No silk curtains. The wallpaper didn't match, and the divan was an iron bedstead in the back room, with a patchwork quilt instead of a leopard skin. The bedstead had the paint knocked off in spots. She came back with the drinks on a tray—straight whiskey in glasses that would fit snugly on your thumb. We each took one, raised it in a silent toast—to the devil, I supposed—and downed it. And right then I wondered what heinous crime I had ever committed that I should be subjected to such punishment as this. When that fiery stuff started down my throat I shut my eyes, bowed my head, and clinched my fists. As soon as I recovered my breath, I glanced through my tears at another young fellow sitting opposite me. He looked at me and we both grinned....

"I waited a few minutes and then I ordered a round of drinks. Mustn't let 'em think I was trying to break up the party. By this time some were dancing and more girls were coming in—the chances of starting that bunch for home seemed slim. As I look back on it now I can honestly say that few, if any, of the crowd were having fun. It was all in the order of refusing a dare. No one but a confirmed alcoholic could possibly have enjoyed that stuff we were served. And the younger ones did not have the courage to decline....

"Anchorage was a disappointment to these women as well as to those in legitimate businesses and occupations. The low scale established by the government stopped all chances of quick easy money, so when Riley came through and announced the discovery of gold on the Tolstoi, a stampede started and these women flocked to the new diggings."

Kenneth Gideon, the "wandering boy," was not far behind. After a brief stint of working in one of the Willow Creek gold mines north of Anchorage, he too mushed on to Tolstoi. ■

Cordova Daily Times

"UNPREJUDICED VIEW OF THE SITUATION AT ANCHORAGE*

Cordova—June 29, 1915

"Mr. George C. Hazelet returned yesterday from a week's visit to Anchorage observing the conditions there and moving around the country somewhat. A representative of the *Times* interviewed Mr. Hazelet this morning to secure the impressions of the new town and Mr. Hazelet talked freely about the railroad work there and the possibilities of the country. He said: 'I went to Anchorage to investigate the conditions in the town for my own satisfaction and to size up the business at first hand.

"'I found the largest tent town I ever saw—from 2,000 to 2,500 people are fed, housed, and their wants, in a way, taken care of in tents, all located on the government railway terminal ground.

"'There are from 25 to 30 restaurants and as many lodging houses, ranging from 8x10 to 16x34 feet. There are from 13 to 16 places where groceries are sold, running from peanut stands with sugar, coffee and the staples up to fair stocks of groceries, including fresh vegetables and fruits, and more are coming in with each boat. There are two or three places where men's furnishings goods are sold in conjunction with hardware, etc., and as many dry goods and ladies' furnishings places. The town has 15 or 20 barber shops and one bath tent, six laundries, two watch and clock repair shops, three tin shops, five transfer outfits, two drug stores, one sawmill, one picture show, one newspaper, several lawyers, no saloons—but plenty of booze, ten cigar stores, several real estate and brokerage firms. Numerous other small businesses are represented.

"'There are 600 to 700 men out of work. The railway officials tell me they employ 1,000 men in all capacities. The work is strung along 20 miles from Anchorage towards the Matanuska River let out in station work. The right of way is cleared beyond that for some distance. Common labor is 37.5 cents an hour for eight hours work, with a shut down on Sunday. Carpenters receive 40 to 60 cents per hour.

"'It is said to be the intention of the government to dredge out a dock, with lock. This is necessary because of the extreme tide of 42.6 feet, the second highest in the world, and the ice conditions that prevail in the winter.

"'Agents of the government are advertising that Anchorage is to be the ocean terminus, that coal bunkers will be erected and a naval base established. It is evident it is their intention to make an open port the year around if possible. However, this is not believed to be possible by men who are familiar with the conditions. I talked with a number of men, some of whom have lived in Cook's Inlet for the past 36 years and all of whom have operated boats in that section, and they are unanimous in the opinion that it cannot be done. They explain that immense ice gorges pile up clear across the Inlet in an ordinary winter and move back and forth with the tide, sometimes for a distance of 60 miles. The Inlet as a whole does not freeze over, hence it is not a question for an ice breaker, but the ice and snow freezes in masses 10 to 15 feet thick and move back and forth from 5 to 11 miles per hour, owing to the stage of the tide.

"'My observations were that boats are required to wait for the tide to go in any direction from Anchorage. In fact, the book says that sea-going vessels should not attempt to go over the bar between Fire Island and McKenzie Point at less than half tide. To go to Knik Arm from Anchorage one must wait until the tide is flooding, and to get out of the Arm one must wait until it ebbs. The same applies to Turnagain Arm. Leaving Anchorage for Turnagain Arm, one must go out on the ebb tide and lie back of Fire Island until the tide turns and go up the Arm with the flood, and then reverse this to get back.

"'It is said that 300 homesteads have been taken up from Anchorage up the Matanuska, and in and around Knik. An examination of the ground at Anchorage, Hope, and Sunrise showed a deposit of a light alluvial soil from six inches to one foot in depth, underlaid with gravel. The soil appears very productive for vegetables, but in dry weather it is so light it blows away very rapidly, similar to all the soil in all sections of Alaska, so far as my observations have extended.

"'Dissatisfaction on all sides is rife at Anchorage. This, however, is common to all big new enterprises. There seem to be several bones of contention between the people and the government officials, such as low wages, short hours, employment of foreigners, discrimination against Americans, etc. The principal objection offered, however, seems to be against the method of handling the town site. The fact that any one individual may purchase all the lots, or as many as he likes, and that these may be transferred to other parties, opens a good way for speculation and pooling, and prevents the man of small means from getting a foothold in the town. Nothing is discussed so much these days in Anchorage as the town site problem. I quote what you hear on the street anywhere: "Here is a mass of 2,000 people squatted on the government terminals from which they soon must move, many of them with just enough money to build a small building and start their business, forced to bid against some fellow from the states who has plenty of money and desires to speculate. This is un-American, and directly opposed to the avowed policy of the administration. Why is it done?"

"'I was told that a petition signed by 2,000 had been sent to President Wilson on June 27th, protesting against the disposition of the lots to the highest bidder, without restriction as to number or building clauses.

"'The conclusion I arrived at after a week's examination of the town situation, was that during the construction period of the railway, Anchorage will do a fairly good business in a small way; that after the road is completed, Anchorage will be the ocean terminus for governmental operations seven or eight months of each year, and that the balance of the year there will be but little business. I arrived at this conclusion because, from the best information I could obtain, it will not be possible to maintain an all the year around ocean service. I obtained the information from men that have spent 15 to 25 years in Cook's Inlet, and whose interests are there.

"'The amount of tonnage to be shipped from the port must necessarily depend on future development, for at the present time there is absolutely none in sight save a possible 125,000 tons of coal annually for naval use on the Pacific, and this amount is gradually being reduced each year by the replacement of coal by oil as a fuel. To my mind this condition will create a serious problem for the operating engineer of the government railway, and that problem will be how to make railway pay even operating expenses when it is completed.'" ■

*Authors Note: Although George Cheever Hazelet, the Cordova town site manager, could hardly be considered "unprejudiced," his observations were generally factual.

3

A Railroad Town

Anchorage's early red light district, "the Line," was located within Chugach National Forest where residents were required to obtain camping permits from the U.S. Forest Service.

Neither William Edes nor Lt. Frederick Mears wished to become deeply involved in running the town. They were in Alaska to build a railroad. Although civic government was outside of their experience, the Alaska Engineering Commission assumed responsibility for sanitation and fire protection. Therefore, they had to contend with providing other services: lighting, telephone, and sewer and water systems. Initially the A.E.C. power plant was able to supply electricity, but telephone presented a more difficult problem. Prior to the auction, a stampeder had shipped up telephone equipment. He was prepared to install it but he discovered that he needed permission from Washington, D.C. before he could string lines. In October, when Secretary of the Interior Lane finally authorized the Commission to install telephones, Mears relieved an embarrassing situation by purchasing the equipment from the would-be entrepreneur.

All Anchorage residents and businesses depended on outhouses until 1917, when a sewer system was installed for the central area. Residences outside the central area still had their backyard facilities, like those described by Lilian Rivers Stolt. "The first spring after we arrived in Anchorage, Father built another outhouse in the back yard. He said, 'Too much competition with the women of this house. I'm building one for myself.' He told us never to use his outhouse—and that was an order! So we became the first house in Anchorage with two outhouses instead of a home with one two-holer outhouse. The following winter we had our own sauna in the backyard. At last we didn't have to walk across town to take a bath!"

Schools were another problem; they were inadvertently omitted from the list of specific services for which the Commission could assess Anchorage lots. Furthermore, territorial funds were inadequate for the needs of a community as large as Anchorage. The legislature was forbidden by the Alaska Organic Act of 1912 from enacting special school laws. The governor was reluctant to use Nelson-law funds, which were collected by taxing fish processors and designed to help small, scattered non-Native settlements—not a government metropolis with about 200 school-age children. The Commission appealed to both Secretary Lane and Governor Strong—neither would relent until the harassed school board threatened to close schools unless teachers could be paid. Lane relented and Edes appointed Andrew Christensen to assume operation of the school while Commission money was being used for maintenance. Finally, on April 17, 1917, Congress passed an act allowing fifty percent of the money from sales of lots to be used for school construction. Congress also repealed the restrictions regarding schools imposed on the territorial legislature. Working with Christensen, the legislature enacted a bill giving unincorporated towns with at least thirty school-age children the right to elect a school board that could evaluate real and personal property and levy a tax of up to one percent of the valuation. The Commission completed the new school with construction costs reimbursed by the "fifty percent fund."

The Commission had even greater problems keeping Anchorage free from the evil three—alcohol, prostitution, and gambling. Prostitutes were tolerated, but restricted to an area on the outskirts of town. Land surrounding the town site was still in the Chugach Na-

Anchorage Museum of History and Art

Ships were unable to dock in Anchorage. Passengers came ashore in shallow draft boats.

41

tional Forest and foresters complained about issuing camping permits to prostitutes.

The Commission wanted to control gambling through law enforcement rather than property confiscation. When local federal marshals did not provide sufficiently diligent surveillance, Christensen decided to conduct his own raid on a gambling den with the help of the assistant district attorney and an out-of-town deputy marshal. On November 17, 1916, Christensen and his band descended upon a pool hall named "The Bank" and arrested fourteen dealers and players. Arrest was easier than conviction. The defendants hired Seward attorney L.V. Ray, who was noted for dramatic court appearances. The *Anchorage Daily Times* reported on December 12 that the Moose Hall had been hired to accommodate the crowds that filled the hall "almost to suffocation to hear the much-talked-of and much-advertised gambling cases that are now being tried with Judge Leopold David in the position of the just judge." After the jury failed to convict the defendants, who had also been unsuccessfully tried in November, Anchorage residents applauded the Commission's decision to drop further attempts at prosecution. The *Seward Gateway* reported on December 19, "L.V. Ray has returned from Anchorage after having been lionized at Anchorage for his successful fight on behalf of the men charged with gambling." In the meantime, the Commission obtained more diligent surveillance by persuading the Justice Department to transfer the lax deputy marshal to Matanuska and replace him with the Matanuska deputy who had participated in the raid.

The announcement on December 15, 1916, that 3,820 bottles of whiskey and 814 bottles of beer bound for Anchorage, which had been seized by federal officials at Point Campbell on Knik Arm, were to be sold at public auction at Seward under the auspices of the district attorney and U.S. Marshal's offices stimulated comment from editors of both Anchorage and Seward papers. The *Seward Gateway* promptly came to the defense of local saloons. "The only people wronged are the men who pay that

Men, horses, and a steam shovel build railbed at Mile 104 in September 1916. Many steam shovels used to build the Alaska Railroad had seen service digging the Panama Canal.

thousand a year and, after all, their business cannot be so very vile when Uncle Sam himself adopts it as a profession. As long as you are taking their money, Uncle, why sell your poison to the people direct." The *Anchorage Daily Times* editor commented on

December 18: "The sale of liquor places the government in rather an anomalous position, in this, that while in the sacred limits of the town site of Anchorage the sale of liquors is prohibited, we find the same government prepared to itself engage in the sale of intoxicating liquors in a neighboring community....It would appear that if it were wrong to sell intoxicating liquors in one community, it would be equally wrong to sell them in another. But it often occurs that Uncle Sam's right hand does not know, or realize, what his left hand is doing." On December 15, the sale was postponed for at least a week, and on December 27, the Seward editor questioned, "Who ever got the idea anyway of taking whiskey from saintly Anchorage and feeding it to the benighted people of Seward? What brilliant government mentality conceived the project?" Early in January 1917, Delegate Wickersham proposed the Alaska Bone Dry Law in Congress. Review of the Seward papers through January provided no evidence that the much-heralded public liquor sale ever actually took place.

While Anchorage experienced growing pains, the world faced more serious problems. Even before the United States entered World War I, the 1916 preparedness boom drew men from the railroad. A shortage of unskilled labor hampered construction after 1917, the A.E.C.'s peak employment year. By the summer of 1918, the working force averaged 2,800 compared to 5,675 in 1917. Mears resigned in January 1918 to accept a colonelcy and command of the 31st Engineer Regiment. Many of the Commission's clerical and engineering forces left with him. As soon as railroad construction between Seward and Anchorage was completed in October 1918, Edes moved his headquarters to Anchorage, effectively eliminating the Seward division.

The influenza epidemic followed in 1919. William Edes was one of the first to catch the flu and resigned on August 29, 1919. Mears, who returned to Alaska at Secretary Lane's request, assumed the dual role of chairman and chief engineer. As one of his first acts, he issued a reorganization circular calling for a Southern Division south of Broad Pass and a Northern Division from Broad Pass to Fairbanks.

Anchorage Museum of History and Art

In its infancy, Anchorage consumed vast amounts of lumber and wood.

The scope given to the Anchorage-based Southern division presaged the centralization of all railroad administration in Anchorage. The original appropriation of $35 million ran out in 1919. Additional appropriations of $17 million and $4 million brought the final railroad construction cost to $56 million.

During the A.E.C.'s administration, Anchorage evolved from a rough construction camp into an established railroad town with a hospital, a dock, electricity, sewers, and a school. Many Anchorage citizens were content with Commission government, but government officials began to consider phasing out city management. As early as December 1915, Andrew Christensen stated, "Personally, I should think it would be a good idea to always have in mind the withdrawal from the management of these towns, so that it can be done gracefully and with dignity." ■

45

Joe Spenard's Legacy

Joe Spenard, a Valdez pushcart peddler, came to Anchorage in 1916 to seek his fortune. Although he encountered more misfortune than success and left town after a few years, his name is still ingrained on a large part of urban Anchorage.

A showman at heart, Joe decked himself out in a garish yellow suit and top hat, plastered his slogan, "Time and Tide will Not Wait, But City Express Is Never Late," on the radiator of his Reo truck, and went into the motorized transfer business. He took special delight in packing the Reo with as many Anchorage youngsters as would fit and hauling them around town. Cutting

Anchorage Museum of History and Art / Alaska Railroad Collection

Joe Spenard left a lasting legacy for Anchorage with what became the Lake Spenard Recreational area. These residents are enjoying its cool waters in 1916.

and hauling wood was a lucrative aspect of his transfer business. Joe was looking for a wood source when he discovered a scenic lake south of town. Actually this lake was already unofficially named for Thomas Jeter, who had lived in a lakeside cabin for five years. The lake was in the Chugach National Forest and not open to homesteading at the time, so Jeter lost a court battle to keep his cabin. Nevertheless, Joe Spenard developed his own plans for the lake and surrounding land.

He needed an access road, so he persuaded members of the Bill's Club, predecessor of the Anchorage Elk's Club, to help him. Together they cut trees and built a corduroy trail from the city boundary at Ninth Avenue and L Street across Chester and Fish Creek valleys to the lake. Then he cleared a portion of the lake shore for a dance pavilion.

Although the Forest Service informed Spenard that cutting trees and building facilities in the Chugach National Forest was illegal, the lake and dance pavilion soon became popular with Anchorage residents. The dance pavilion burned in May 1917. Shortly thereafter, Spenard broke his leg and developed a heart condition that prompted him to sell his transfer business and move to Sacramento, California, where he died in 1934.

The lake continued to be a popular winter and summer recreational site for residents. At the request of the city government, the Forest Service designated the land around the lake for recreational purposes on April 16, 1919. The Elk's Club and the Boy Scouts maintained facilities on the lake until the city established a park and hired staff to supervise maintenance and concessions. Spenard Lake continues to be used for recreation but is best known as part of Anchorage's large float-plane base. Spenard Road follows the early trail to the lake and the area through which it passes is still called Spenard although it is all part of the Municipality of Anchorage. ∎

In 1923, Warren G. Harding became the first president of the United States to visit Alaska. Harding came north to commemorate the completion of the Alaska Railroad.

4

The End of the Boom

Alaska Railroad

President Warren G. Harding drives in the final spike of the Alaska Railroad near Nenana. Anchorage was now connected with Fairbanks in the north and Seward to the south.

W orld War I and the influenza epidemic ended the Anchorage railroad construction boom. The population, estimated at 6,000 in 1916, dropped to less than 2,000 in 1920. Labor shortages slowed construction because men who left to fight did not return after the war. The Alaska Engineering Commission persuaded reluctant Anchorage citizens to assume responsibility for local government but retained many of the essential functions such as the port and medical facilities. Even after the railroad was completed between Seward and Fairbanks, it did not live up to its promise as a way to open the surrounding land to settlement. Anchorage population at the end of 1929 was 2,277—an increase of only 421 during the ten-year period.

In the spring of 1920, the Alaska Engineering Commission and a Chamber of Commerce committee began to work towards establishing a plan for civilian control. Earlier influential businessmen had opposed a greater degree of home rule because they feared increased taxation if federal supports were withdrawn upon incorporation. Initially the two sides disagreed on the amount that the A.E.C. would turn over to a new government. The Chamber insisted on receiving unsold and forfeited lots as well as permission to tax the residences owned by the Commission. The A.E.C. offered to give the city only the schoolhouse, firehouse, water mains, streets, and a block for municipal buildings. The stalemate was broken at a mass meeting when the A.E.C. chief accountant made it clear that the federal government would no longer provide fire protection. Even though they complained about "bureaucratic domination," Anchorage residents barely passed the vote for incorporation. On November 23, 1920, the federal district judge signed the court order declaring Anchorage legally incorporated. At the election, the voters selected a seven-member city council, which subsequently designated Leopold David as mayor under the weak-mayor form of government authorized by territorial law.

Once they were divested of the problems of city administration, railroad officials were free to concentrate on completing the railroad. Mears assumed full charge after William Edes' resignation and President Wilson's appointment of Thomas Riggs as governor of Alaska. On November 26, 1921, the first excursion train ran from Seward to Fairbanks. During the next two years, steel bridges were finished and citizens of the Railbelt prepared for the first presidential visit to the Territory.

Amid blaring bands and cheers of thousands, President and Mrs.

Warren G. Harding, along with Secretary of the Interior Hubert Work, Secretary of Commerce Herbert Hoover, and Secretary of Agriculture Henry Wallace, and their wives, sailed from Tacoma on July 6, 1923, aboard the transport *Henderson*. A week later the party arrived in Anchorage and boarded an Alaska Railroad train for Nenana, where President Harding drove the golden spike symbolizing the railroad's completion. Governor Scott Bone carefully inserted the spike in the hole prepared for it and Harding tapped it gently with a hammer. The spike was then withdrawn and a plain iron spike substituted. The people of Anchorage bought the golden spike, made of 14-carat gold and valued at $600, as a gift to Colonel Mears, although he was no longer associated with the railroad. The Harding administration combined the railroad administration with the Alaska Road Commission under the direction of James G. Steese in an effort to consolidate federal agencies involved in Alaskan transportation. Steese, who accepted the chairmanship of the railroad from Mears in Anchorage on May 1, 1923, accompanied the presidential party during the Alaska trip.

The presidential party spent several additional days in Alaska, visiting Cordova and viewing the spectacular glaciers from the Copper River and Northwestern Railroad. Alaskans hoped Harding's visit would educate him about problems in the territory, but shortly after returning from the trip, Harding died suddenly and was replaced by Vice President Calvin Coolidge.

In addition to maintenance problems on the railroad, the Steese administration was impeded by discontent in Anchorage because the railroad failed to stimulate an economic boom. Discontent was simmering before Steese arrived, but Mears had enjoyed the loyalty of railroad employees and the confidence of Anchorage businessmen. Steese developed connections with river boats at Nenana and started Golden Belt Tours, using the Copper River and Northwestern Railroad and Richardson Highway along with the Alaska Railroad. Congress recognized that the differing natures of railroad and highway administration would cause internal problems. On September 29, 1923, Interior Secretary Work announced that Steese would resume the presidency of the Board of Road Commissioners while Lee H. Landis, a veteran railroader, would fill the newly created position of railroad general manager. In an attempt to make the railroad an economic success, on the surface at least, Landis cut maintenance funding and fired key employees, prompting Governor Bone to appeal to Secretary Work for a resolution to the railroad problems. On July 7, 1924, Work appointed Noel W. Smith, a veteran executive with the Pennsylvania Railroad, to be "Special Assistant to the Secretary of the Interior" and recommend necessary changes.

Smith came to Alaska intending to stay a few months, but remained four years. He assumed active control of the Alaska Railroad in August, and Landis officially resigned on November 11. Smith worked closely with Secretary Work and President Coolidge, who

In Alaska, the traditional and the modern frequently meet. Note how the dogs are hitched to the train.

felt that more than enough federal money was already going to Alaska and that neither Alaska's prospects nor the quality of its population justified an increase. Although Smith followed a policy of strict economy, he spent money on permanent improvements as long as they would reduce maintenance costs. He did not, however, believe that the railroad should subsidize economic development. Closing the port of Anchorage was one of Smith's earliest and most controversial decisions. During the seven months that the port was open, steamship companies could haul freight to the Cook Inlet port more cheaply than the railroad could carry it from Seward. Railroad wharfage fees were considerably less than the potential income of the line

Alaska and Polar Regions Archives, Rasmuson Library, University of Alaska Fairbanks

haul from Seward. By closing the port and forcing all freight to come through the port of Seward, Smith effectively raised freight costs for Anchorage residents and businesses. He maintained the dock in reasonable shape so it could be utilized in emergencies—such as blockage of the railroad south of Anchorage. In the spring of 1927, Smith and the Anchorage City Council agreed to share the cost of a supplementary dock at the mouth of Ship Creek for small boat trading in the Cook Inlet area.

The government continued to provide medical care in Anchorage. The rest of Alaska also benefited from the services of the railroad physician, Dr. J.B. Beeson, as demonstrated by the following front page article in the January 25, 1925, *Alaska Daily Empire* in Juneau: "ANCHORAGE, Jan. 23—Three thousand units of diphtheria antitoxin left yesterday on the Alaska Railroad train for Nenana and relays of the fastest dog teams in Alaska will carry the serum to Nome, through temperature ranging from 40 to 54 degrees below zero. The serum was supplied by Dr. J.B. Beeson, who made a 600 mile race against death in 1920 by dog team to the Iditarod."

Access to the Matanuska coal fields was one of the original justifications for building the Alaska Railroad and the spur line to bring coal to the bunkers at the Ship Creek port, but tests of the coal for naval use in 1922 were disappointing. Furthermore, the Navy was finding it advantageous to modify their boilers to burn oil that could be provided more cheaply from California wells. The Navy coal reserve at Chickaloon was abandoned in 1923 and some of its buildings were moved to Anchorage. The rail spur continued to transport coal from nearby private mines to supply fuel for the railroad and Anchorage buildings.

Gold mining, which started in the Talkeetna Mountains north of Anchorage at the turn of the century, continued throughout the 1920s. Lucky Shot and War Baby mines in the Craigie Creek Valley were the main producers until the Lucky Shot stamp mill burned in 1924. Rising mining costs added to the slump in gold production. A brief flurry of oil speculation around Kanatak on the east side of the Alaska Peninsula in 1924 and 1925 failed to result in any producing oil wells. The only part of Alaska that was enjoying an economic boom during the 1920s was

Anchorage Museum of History and Art

Members of the Los Angeles Chamber of Commerce tee off on Anchorage's first golf course in a visit when the city was less than ten years old.

the Copper River area where the Kennecott copper mines were producing high grade copper ore carried to Cordova on the Copper River and Northwestern Railroad.

The depressed Alaska economy did not lure many settlers north. A few homesteads in the Matanuska Valley continued to supply vegetables for the Willow Creek mines. In the Anchorage area, the Martin family's Step and a Half Ranch produced milk for sale in town. After the Chugiak-Eagle River area was removed from the Chugach National Forest in 1919, John Siebenthaler, who had come to Alaska as a shop foreman at the Chickaloon coal mine, filed on a homestead that included Lower Fire Lake. His brother Frank came north to join him and filed on adjacent land to establish a mink farm. Since there were no roads in the area, the families commuted to jobs in Anchorage on the railroad.

Bootlegging and prostitution continued to be underground industries during the 1920s. Anchorage children were offered $5 rewards for revealing the whereabouts of illicit stills, while respectable families produced their own home brew. Bill Stolt described his mother's solution to the alcohol problem. "She bought a five gallon crock and collected some bottles. She also bought some hops, malt syrup, and a bottle capper.

Then she cooked up a batch of home brew, bottled it, and put it in the cellar. When it was ready for drinking, she casually remarked that there was home brew in the cellar, and that I could invite the boys over to our house to have some home brew without paying fifty cents a cup....I was never much of a home brew drinker and by having it on tap at home, mother took the thrill out of buying at a speakeasy."

Young Frank M. Reed, whose mother ran the Anchorage Hotel, developed his own home industry by collecting bottles discarded by hotel guests, washing them, and selling them to bootleggers for thirty-five cents a dozen, washed. He also earned money selling newspapers in the hotel lobby and delivering papers to the girls on the Line on Ninth Avenue between B Street and Barrow. These youthful entrepreneurial activities prepared Frank for a subsequent career as an Anchorage banker and community leader.

Young Frank's father, Frank I. Reed, one of Anchorage's first city councilmen, was a self-made financial success and community leader during the 1920s. After gold-mining in Nome in 1903, starting a dredge operation at Cache Creek in 1913, and timber cutting in Southcentral Alaska in 1915, he settled in Anchorage and started a lumber yard. He acquired the Anchorage Hotel to settle a lumber yard debt, but left hotel management to his wife while pursuing another lifelong concern, the Eklutna Power Plant. John J. Longacre, an electrical engineer with the Alaska Railroad, had conceived the idea that hydroelectric power production from the Eklutna Lake source was feasible, but promotion of the project was accomplished largely by Reed, whose application to the Federal Power Commission was approved March 8, 1923. He was issued a license to undertake power development and went to San Francisco, where he raised $750,000 for the project. Construction started in July of 1928 and full-time production began in January 1930.

Bill and Lily Stolt described their experiences growing up and courting in Anchorage during the twenties in their book, *Bill and Lily, Two Alaskans*. Bill was one of the few young men who owned a car, a Ford, which he decorated with flowers as a float in Anchorage parades. The only two roads out of downtown Anchorage were the four-mile trail to Lake Spenard and a twenty-two-mile tree-lined gravel loop through the wilderness north of town where the military bases are now located. Cars were stored on blocks during the winter because there was no snow removal on the city streets. Anchorage young people walked to Lake Spenard to swim in the summer and skated on Spenard and Otis Lakes in the winter. Both Bill and Lilian's families were Finnish, and many of their social activities took place in the Suomi social hall. Cap Lathrop's Empress Theater, which housed both silent movies and town meetings, was another popular gathering spot for early Anchorage residents. Lily used a crystal set with earphones and bedsprings for an antenna to listen to the new radio station, KFQD, which started broadcasting in 1924.

Anchorage residents prepared to welcome a new form of transportation when bush pilots started to fly small open-cockpit airplanes in Alaska. Since planes needed a place to land, townspeople turned out in May 1923 to clear the land between Ninth and Tenth Avenues and C and L Streets, which had originally been dedicated as a firebreak to keep fires from coming into downtown Anchorage from the south. The *Anchorage Daily Times* described the May 27 event: "Men whose hands had not been soiled by anything heavier than a pen for many years, grappled the mattock or the axe and shook the kinks out of their flabby muscles. Ladies with rakes and other implements cleared away the small debris while others piled it upon the small mountain of stumps ready for the torch."

Two days later, the people celebrated with a barbecue. Anchorage had its first aviation field, but it was another year before it was put to use by Noel Wien. In June 1924, he brought a "J-One" standard plane over the railroad from Seward and assembled it in Anchorage to give local residents joyrides. Lily Stolt recalls seeing one small plane that missed the field and landed in the crossbeam of a nearby telephone pole. "The pilot was not hurt; he just climbed down the pole to the ground."

The Park Strip was home to the first local airline company, Anchorage Air Transport, Inc., formed in 1926 by Art Shonbeck, Oscar Anderson, Gus Gelles, and Ray Southworth, with Russ Merrill as their first pilot. The Park Strip was used as an aviation field for about seven years and then became the first town golf course. Even after Merrill Field was completed in 1929, spring breakup sometimes forced pilots to use the more solid town strip. ∎

Alaska's Most Famous Painter

Sydney Mortimer Laurence was one of the unique assortment of men with mysterious past lives who came north seeking gold at the start of the twentieth century. Laurence was born in Brooklyn, New York, on October 14, 1865 and attended Peekskill Military Academy before, reportedly, running away to sea.

By 1887, Laurence was painting and exhibiting his works in New York City, having studied art with Edward Moran. Several noted artists, including Thomas Moran, attended his wedding to artist Alexandrina Dupres in New York on May 18, 1889.

The young couple immediately sailed for England and settled at St. Ives in Cornwall. Laurence exhibited paintings in England and France and won honorable mention for a "marine" at the Paris Salon. In 1894, he was an illustrator-correspondent in Africa where he may have sustained a blow to the left ear resulting in hearing loss. He continued his career as an artist correspondent in the Spanish-American War, the Boer War, and the Boxer Rebellion in China.

Anchorage Museum of History and Art

Sydney Mortimer Laurence

Although *Black and White* magazine continued to feature Laurence's work, he apparently left London in 1903, leaving his wife and sons, Leslie, age eight, and Eugene, age one. Christmas postcards sent to their father at Tyoonok [sic], Alaska, in 1904 were the only communications between Laurence and his family. While Laurence stayed with Durrel Finch at the Alaska Commercial Company in Tyonek, he painted pictures of the area and filed mining claims in the Talkeetna recording district. In 1909 he moved on to Cordova and painted in the studio of photographer Eric Hegg. Before settling in Valdez in December 1912, Laurence prospected and painted at Beluga, Seldovia, and Ninilchik.

A company, formed in Valdez, sent Laurence to make sketches of Mount McKinley and produce a painting to exhibit at the Panama Pacific exhibition in San Francisco. The following summer he camped south of the mountain and passed through Knik in October on his way back to Valdez. The resulting painting, *Top of the Continent*, was accessioned into the National Collection of Fine Arts, Smithsonian Institution, on February 25, 1915.

Laurence moved to Anchorage in June 1915 and opened a studio for "commercial and pictorial photography" on the corner of Fourth Avenue and E Street. A year later he moved his office to the Harmony Theatre. When he was not mining in the Cache Creek area near Talkeetna, Laurence lived in the Anchorage Hotel. Belle Simpson, owner of the Nugget Shop in Juneau, began selling Laurence's paintings in 1919, and he was soon recognized as Alaska's most prominent painter.

The decorative titles that Laurence painted for the silent film melodrama *The Cheechakos* introduced his work beyond Alaska, and he opened a studio in Los Angeles in 1924. For the rest of his life, he spent winters in California and summers in Anchorage. He continued to supply paintings for Belle Simpson to sell at the Nugget Shop, and Carl Block of Peoria, Illinois ordered paintings to sell in his department stores throughout the 1930s.

When Leslie Frederick Laurence married in England in 1926, he was said to be the "son of Mrs. Alex Laurence and the late Mr. Sydney Laurence." Sydney, on the other hand, identified himself as a widower when he married Jeanne Kunuth Holeman in Los Angeles in October 1928. Laurence continued to paint in Los Angeles, Seattle, and Anchorage until 193,1 when he suffered a slight stroke that affected his coordination. When Alexandrina Laurence died in England in 1935, her death certificate listed her as the widow of Sydney Laurence, who subsequently died at Providence Hospital in Anchorage on September 13, 1940—demonstrating that Alaska and England were worlds apart. ■

Judge Leopold David—Anchorage's First Mayor

Anchorage citizens chose Leopold David to be their first mayor after the Alaska Engineering Commission turned over the new city's management to civilian government. David was born in Nordhausen, Germany in 1881 to Jewish parents, who emigrated to New York with their five children. After his parents died in the mid-1890s, Leopold enlisted in the Army and served in the Philippines during the rebellious aftermath of the Spanish-American War.

Sergeant First Class David arrived in Alaska in September 1904, assigned to Fort Egbert at Eagle as a pharmacist's assistant in the Hospital Corps. Upon discharge in 1905, he settled in Seward, where he became manager of the Seward Drug Company. Like many pharmacists of the time, his knowledge of medicine earned him the title of "Dr. David" and newspaper advertisements listed him as "Physician and Surgeon."

In 1909 when he moved to Susitna Station to serve as United States Marshal. A year later, he settled in Knik and was appointed U.S. Commissioner, a post that he held until 1921. As Commissioner, he recorded deeds and mining claims and served as ex-officio probate judge. In the meantime, he studied law and became a member of the Washington State Bar. In 1921, he joined Seward attorney L.V. Ray in private law practice and ran the firm's Anchorage office.

David arrived at Ship Creek in May 1915 and attended the July 10 auction, where he acquired two city lots. In addition to the Commissioner's office, one lot housed offices of the Alaska Publishing Company, of which David was a trustee. David was active in community affairs in both Knik and Anchorage, including the Chamber of Commerce and several fraternal organizations: the Elks, the Moose Lodge, the Shriners, and the Masons. On November 29, 1920, he was elected to the first of two terms as mayor of Anchorage.

One of the first tasks confronting the new government was property assessment. The city council adopted ordinances which mandated businesses to shovel snow from sidewalks in downtown blocks; "male and female youths under sixteen" to obey a 9 p.m. to 5 a.m. curfew; motor vehicles to be provided with lights; the legal speed limit in town to be eight miles per hour; and prohibited expectorating in public places. To discourage gambling, the council adopted a "curtain ordinance" requiring an unobstructed view from the street into "pool halls, cigar stores, soft-drink emporiums, and other businesses of a similar character." Although prohibition had been adopted in 1918, it was virtually impossible to keep alcohol out of town, and Judge David was forced to hand down stiff sentences to bootleggers. After a crackdown on illegal stills in town, the police chief was shot to death in the alley between Fourth and Fifth Avenues. A few weeks later, a gunman held up the Bank of Alaska in broad daylight.

Judge David left the council after his second term and devoted himself to his law practice. He died of heart failure on November 21, 1924 leaving his wife, Anna, and two children, Caroline and Leopold Jr. Judge Leopold David's headstone in the Anchorage Municipal Cemetery erroneously identifies him as "Physician and Surgeon" rather than as "Attorney at Law." ■

Anchorage Museum of History and Art

Thanks to the Army engineers, who laid out the town site, Anchorage had wide avenues and streets even as early as 1916.

"The Cheechakos"
Alaska's Home-Grown Motion Picture

Anchorage Museum of History and Art

Action builds in the log dance hall in Alaska's motion picture, "The Cheechakos."

For several years motion pictures about Alaska, based on books by Jack London and Rex Beach, had thrilled audiences, but they were all filmed in other locations. When a group of Portland, Oregon promoters toured Alaskan towns in the summer of 1922 with a plan to produce a travelogue and feature film in Alaska, Alaskan businessmen welcomed the opportunity to publicize the territory and organized fund-raising committees in Seward, Anchorage, Fairbanks, Nenana, and Cordova. They formed the Alaska Motion Picture Corporation and elected Captain

Austin E. Lathrop, who owned picture theaters in all those cities, president. Stock sales raised $75,000 to produce a twelve-reel picture—a three-reel travelogue, filmed in participating towns, followed by a nine-reel drama.

Anchorage looked forward to becoming the "Hollywood of the North." On November 13, 1922, construction started on a 7,000-square-foot moving picture studio in downtown Anchorage. A thousand Anchorage residents greeted the cast of artists, recruited in Portland, New York, and Hollywood, with a "free dance and jollification at the moviedome." Taking advantage of the opportunity, the director mounted a platform and filmed several hundred couples dancing.

After a short rest, the cast and production crew boarded the Alaska Railroad for McKinley National Park, where they filmed winter scenes with

Anchorage Museum of History and Art

Actors, playing Alaskan gold seekers, mill around the movie set for "The Cheechakos."
Some of the actors had originally come to Alaska as gold miners.

dog teams to accompany the drama depicting gold rush days. The picture crew then took a private train to Girdwood, the small mining town on Turnagain Arm chosen to represent Skagway. The *Anchorage Daily Times* provided the following description on April 4, 1923:

"Six moving picture cameras will be swung into use to catch every phase of the gigantic repetition of the days of '97 and '98 showing a thousand camp fires, glowing softly through the night at the base of a lofty mountain pass, while impatient chechacoes [*sic*] and grizzled, bewhiskered sourdoughs strut around the town anxiously waiting the break of dawn, signaling the rush of gold-seekers over the towering pass.

"The struggles of former years will once again be fought by real veterans of the early days, many of them still retaining and wearing the identical garments and packs, such as jackets, parkas, fur hats and pack boards used by their owners during the stampede days over the great Chilkoot Pass. Tandem dog teams will once again hit the trail with the Yukon sled in prominence. The vast illumination will portray sled loads of supplies of flour, bacon, salt, beans, sugar, coffee, tobacco, and other bare necessities used by the prospectors.

"The first unit of the great gold rush will terminate a week later at Mile 52, where 300 people, consisting of the cast, assistants, Anchorageites and other Alaskan folks, will cross the mountain lying directly back of Bartlett glacier, garbed and outfitted true in the minutest detail to that of 1898."

After filming the winter scenes, the cast returned to Anchorage to shoot interior scenes on four sets constructed in the movie studio and shipboard action on the *Alameda*. The movie crew constructed a log-cabin town on Third Avenue overlooking Cook Inlet for the grand finale of Anchorage filming. On May 23, the *Anchorage Daily Times* explained the fate of this new construction. "The last day on this set will be very spectacular as fire breaks out in the dance hall during the height of festivities, from which the blaze spreads rapidly to the rest of the buildings, wiping out the entire town."

The log cabin village set burned without setting off a general conflagration in Anchorage and the cast departed on June 7 for Cordova to shoot on Eyak Lake, Abercrombie Rapids, and Childs Glacier. Cor-

Gold stampeders in "The Cheechakos" climb up the mountains near Girdwood as they recreate the days of '98 when miners climbed the Chilkoot Pass. Girdwood substituted for Skagway in the only movie ever produced by the Alaska Motion Picture Corporation.

dova, noted for rain, treated the cast with an unprecedented two weeks of sunny weather, during which the glacier calved gigantic icebergs, causing waves that occasionally drenched the cameramen. President Warren Harding rode the Copper River and Northwestern Railroad to visit the production site after driving the final spike on the Alaska Railroad.

During the Cordova filming the Danish leading lady slipped into a crevasse on Childs Glacier and waited four hours before the company could rescue her. Despite six frozen toes, she was enthusiastic about Alaska, and returned to California with a four-month-old bear cub, presented to her in Anchorage; a half-wolf-half-malemute, the gift of Cordova; and 170 logs "ready to be built into a distinctive Hollywood bungalow, reminiscent and typical of Alaska."

The artist Sydney Laurence, who worked as a photographer in Anchorage during the production, provided six paintings used on artistic titles. When the editing was completed, Lathrop took charge of distributing the film. *The Cheechakos* was shown throughout the United States. Critics accepted it as a unique production, praising the scenery but discounting the "silly" story. A *Chicago Tribune* critic described it as, "*The Cheechakos* cooks up a whacking old time melodrama that, in between the play acting, portrays in a way you won't forget the absorbing history of our great northwestern territory. Treachery, shipwreck, a lost child, a betrayed mother, etc., are thrown against natural scenery that makes you catch your breath. Rough men with hearts of gold, gamblers, dance hall girls, dance halls, while used in the unreeling of a movie story, still manage to give you vivid pictures of what the Alaska pioneers did; how they lived; what they were, and the rest of it."

The Cheechakos was not a financial success for Cap Lathrop and his investors. Although they built the movie studio in Anchorage with the intent of producing more films, they soon modified it. The studio and surrounding grounds were transformed into an exhibition center for the Western Alaska Fair over the Labor Day weekend. The building never housed another movie production, but it served as an Anchorage community center for many years. ■

5

Depression Farmers Come North

Colonists from the Midwest prepare to board a train for their new homes in the Matanuska Valley. The Depression-era government program brought experienced farmers to Alaska.

Alaska did not suffer as much as the rest of the country from the 1930s Great Depression, partly because the Alaskan economy had been stagnant during the 1920s. The Copper River area suffered from the Kennecott Mine and the Copper River and Northwestern Railroad closures in 1938. The Anchorage area prospered moderately from federal relief projects, including relocating Midwestern farmers to the Matanuska Valley. An increase in the price of gold resulted in a resurgence of gold mining in the Talkeetna Mountains. Highway and air transport began to compete with the railroad. As the decade closed, increased military construction in preparation for a threatened war with Japan started a new era of prosperity for Anchorage.

Arriving in Washington, D.C., in 1933 to assume his duties, Delegate to Congress Anthony J. Dimond was surprised by the depth of the depression. As a staunch Democrat and supporter of President Franklin D. Roosevelt, he was in a position to make sure Alaska was allowed to participate in at least some of the federal relief projects. Anchorage benefited from construction of a new federal building in 1939; a highway opened to connect the town with an existing network of roads in the Matanuska Valley. Among Civilian Conservation Corps projects was erection of a ski jump at the City Ski Bowl.

The New Deal's most prominent Alaska project relocated 202 families from Minnesota, Wisconsin, and Michigan to farms in the Matanuska Valley north of Anchorage. The federal government wanted to increase Alaska's population for defense purposes and to help farmers in depressed areas. Therefore, the Federal Emergency Rehabilitation Administration endorsed the program to promote farming in Alaska that the railroad manager, Colonel Otto Ohlson, had already started mainly to increase business for the Alaska Railroad.

Ohlson's efforts to entice farmers to Alaska brought few settlers to the Railbelt area prior to the Matanuska colonists' arrival in May 1935. Anchorage residents prepared to welcome the newcomers, but had reservations about the validity of the project. They protested that local labor was not utilized when the federal government recruited more than four hundred "CCC men" from outside of Alaska to set up camps before colonists arrived. Since these transient workers were not paid until they left Alaska, they did nothing to benefit the local economy.

Anchorage enjoyed the nationwide publicity stimulated by the Matanuska colony. Politicians came to praise—or condemn—the colony.

Ernie Pyle stayed with a colonist family for several weeks while gathering material for articles. Rex Beach regretted that the colonists had not been sent to Florida, where they would have an easier life. Will Rogers visited and commented, "Alaska will be all right if she don't let the U.S. take her over. Let her remain Alaskan. I'm coming back here this winter—her winter charms rival those of Switzerland and can be capitalized among tourists for millions." He never made it back; Rogers and Wiley Post died later that same day in a plane crash near Pt. Barrow.

Although some colonists, like Walter Pippel, made money selling produce in Anchorage, the Matanuska cooperative had marketing problems. Local produce was not competitive with foodstuffs shipped from Seattle. Matanuska eggs sold for ten cents more a dozen and milk and cream for five to eight more a quart.

Some colonists left the project to take more lucrative jobs in nearby gold mines. As the price of gold rose during the depression, mines in the Talkeetna Mountains enjoyed a decade of prosperity. A new mill at the Lucky Shot Mine on Craigie Creek—the most productive of the Willow Creek district mines—replaced the mill that burned in 1928. Production from the Lucky Shot War Baby vein decreased in the late 1930s, but the Alaska Pacific Consolidated Mining Corporation undertook major construction at Independence Mine on the other side of the mountain. Since Independence Mine was accessible by road, Anchorage residents started traveling by bus to ski at the mine.

Miners were among the first to appreciate the advantages of air travel in Alaska. Art Shonbeck, an Anchorage mine owner and businessman, had started Anchorage Air Transport in 1926 with Russ Merrill as chief pilot. The new Anchorage airport was named for Merrill, who died in a supply flight to the NYAC mine on the Kuskokwim in 1929. (During the thirties the park strip, which had served as Anchorage's first air strip, became the first city golf course.) By 1935, Bowman Airways, McGee Airways, Star Air Service, and Woodley Airways were operating from Merrill Field. Wesley Earl Dunkle, who realized the value of airplanes while managing the Lucky Shot Mine, was instrumental in starting Star Air Service, the predecessor of Alaska Airlines.

In his efforts to increase Alaska Railroad use, Col. Ohlson waged war with truckers on the Richardson Highway by raising rates on the Tanana River ferry and with steamship operators by charging wharfage fees at the Anchorage port. However, he couldn't do much to compete with the new air transport industry because price competition was not as important. Planes meeting steamships at Seward, Cordova, and Valdez could transport politicians and businessmen, as well as fresh produce, to Anchorage and the Interior more expeditiously than the railroad, which had to cross mountain passes from Seward to Anchorage and then spend a night at Curry before reaching Fairbanks.

In addition to civilian operators, significant military operations based out of Merrill Field. During the summer of 1934, flyers commanded by Lt. Col. "Hap" Arnold used Merrill Field as the base for ten B-10s undertaking aerial reconnaissance of Cook Inlet. The Army Air Corps, under Major Everett S. Davis, used Merrill Field until Elmendorf Field was completed in September 1940.

Throughout the 1930s, Delegate Dimond advocated strengthening North Pacific defenses in Alaska to counteract Japan's military buildup. Brigadier General William Mitchell, who had served in the early 1900s on the construction of the Washington Alaska Military Cable and Telegraph System (WAMCATS), spoke forcefully to Congress in favor of Alaskan air bases in 1935. He predicted the role air power would play in military operations and proclaimed the importance of Alaska's position in the world to come: "Japan is our dangerous enemy in the Pacific. They won't attack Panama. They will come right here to Alaska. Alaska is the most central place in the world for aircraft, and that is true either of Europe, Asia, or North America. I believe, in the future, he who holds Alaska will hold the world."

The next decade would prove the wisdom of Mitchell's foresight! ■

People vs. Pippel

Walter G. Pippel had been a successful truck gardener in Minnesota for fourteen years before he came to the Matanuska Valley in May 1935 with his wife, Melva, and four children. The depression forced him to give up his farm and work as a salesman. His farming experience helped him get a head start on the other colonists and he was selling radishes to Anchorage grocers within weeks of his arrival. As a member of the first board of directors of the Matanuska Valley Farmers' Cooperative Association, he wrote the following testimonial on the valley's agricultural potential in answer to criticism from Senator Elmer Thomas of Oklahoma: "My first year in the Matanuska Valley has thoroughly convinced me that climate, soil and other conditions tend to make this one of the safest and surest spots under the United States flag for a farmer to make his home and ply his vocation....Senator Thomas, the chances are, has never eaten a Matanuska-grown radish. If he had, he couldn't say they taste like icicles. Fine flavor ranks ahead of fine appearance in all the produce I have grown here....I have six acres of garden here that are worth more to me than the 80 acre truck farm I worked for years just outside of Minneapolis."

By 1938, however, Pippel was at odds with the cooperative's administration. He resigned from the board of directors and began criticizing the association's marketing policies because produce grading and sorting were not up to quality that retail stores would accept. When called before the board for selling his vegetables directly rather than using the cooperative, he replied, "I can't afford to bring my good vegetables in here and have them help to sell produce that is inferior. I know how to grow, bunch and sell the produce." Pippel also refused to sign a real estate contract preventing him from selling his land to anyone not associated with the colony.

Pippel hired an attorney and was joined by several other colonists, who agreed the corporation had no right to compel them to market through the cooperative, which was not in existence when they joined the colonization project. Newspapers across the nation carried stories under titles such as "Rugged Individualism versus Government-fostered Co-operative" and "People versus Pippel." Legal maneuvering became so secretive that officials wired their attorneys in Washington, Anchorage, or Seward in code. Lawyers decided to settle out of court, but Secretary Ickes insisted on continuing to prosecute the case. Eventually, Ickes agreed to settle, and Pippel accepted $7,000 with the proviso that he leave Alaska.

When he returned to Minnesota in 1939, Pippel gave reporters a realistic evaluation of farming in Alaska. "Alaska lacks the market. Ten real farmers who got down to brass tacks and dug for their living and for their crop outlets could keep the whole of Alaska supplied with fresh produce." While Pippel was farming in the Matanuska Valley he had developed his own markets in Anchorage, Seward, Cordova, Valdez, and Cook Inlet villages. He'd built a greenhouse and started growing tomatoes to expand his variety of produce.

The Pippel family was sold on Alaska. Two years later they returned and started a hog and vegetable farm in Spenard on Anchorage's outskirts. In 1943, Pippel bought the 160-acre Nyberg homestead in a flat valley on the Palmer Highway north of Anchorage. For a while he managed both the Spenard and Eagle River farms, but in 1948 the family moved to the Nyberg property and the eldest son homesteaded an adjoining eighty-acre tract.

Longtime Anchorage-area residents remember admiring their well-cultivated fifty-acre field and purchasing radishes, turnips, cabbage, lettuce, broccoli, cauliflower, and potatoes at their roadside stand when returning from Matanuska and Susitna Valley cabins.

Walter Pippel continued to farm until he suffered a stroke in the mid-1960s. After his death in 1969, his wife appraised his work. "He had an art about his farming. He was like a poet who writes poems, or a painter who paints pictures. It was born in him. He had that art. Everything he touched would grow." The Pippel children and grandchildren continue to live in Alaska. After they sold the Anchorage-area property to make way for downtown Eagle River, they moved back to the Matanuska Valley. ■

W.E. Dunkle —A Flying Miner

Wesley Earl Dunkle was a leading participant in two of the major activities in Southcentral Alaska during the 1930s. Shortly after graduation from Yale University in 1908 he was employed by the Guggenheim mining syndicate, which sent him to Alaska as field engineer at the Beatson copper mine on Latouche Island in Prince William Sound. After the Beatson mine became part of the Kennecott mining corporation, Dunkle was instrumental in developing the Kennecott mine. As an exploratory mining engineer for Kennecott, he traveled to some of the most remote places in Alaska assessing mining prospects; he also made an extensive visit to South Africa.

Dunkle became convinced of the value of aviation to the mining industry after visiting the Quigley mine at Kantishna in 1928. The trip from the railroad to the mine by dog team had taken two days; a chartered flight back to Fairbanks in a Bennet-Rodebaugh airplane took only two hours. When Dunkle left Kennecott to become manager of the Lucky Shot gold mine in the Willow Creek mining district north of Anchorage for Pardners Mines, he decided to use planes to bring in supplies and workers. During the winter of 1931-32, he started flight training in Seattle but had to return to the mine before he could acquire enough flying hours. Stephen Mills, one of his instructors, expressed an interest in starting an Alaskan flight school, so Dunkle offered to grubstake him. Mills, along with Jack Waterworth and Charlie Ruttan, arrived in Anchorage in March 1932 with a Fleet biplane and went into business as Star Air Service.

Dunkle kept his word about financing the new company and brought in more investors. He also continued his flight lessons and received his private license on September 14, 1932. The newly-licensed pilot promptly purchased a new Travel Air and arranged to fly from New York to Seattle, where it could be disassembled and shipped to Alaska. The eventful cross-country flight involved a crash landing on a Pennsylvania football field. Dunkle eventually got to Alaska with a replacement Travel Air, which he flew on wheels, skis, and floats throughout Alaska until wrecking it on takeoff from Spenard Lake. He also bought and flew a little secondhand Aeronica to get into the small air field that he brushed out at the Lucky Shot mine. He sold this Aeronica to young Bill Egan of Valdez when he bought a new one to replace it. In 1934, Dunkle made a second transcontinental flight to bring a Waco biplane to Alaska from Troy, Ohio. This time he flew the plane from Seattle to Anchorage in a record time of thirteen hours and twenty minutes. When Dunkle was not flying the Waco, Star Airways used it as a standby plane.

Star, which merged with McGee Airways in 1934, kept going back to Dunkle and a small group of investors for loans, and Dunkle continued to supply planes, including a Curtiss Robin on floats. By 1936, Star owned fifteen of the thirty-nine planes based in Anchorage and Fairbanks. Even though air travel was proving its value in Alaska, the infant airlines had a difficult time making a profit and no government subsidies existed until the 1940s. Dunkle, who had a hard time recovering from the death of Stephen Mills in a crash with a party of sightseers in 1936, was disappointed when his partners would not support his efforts to establish regular amphibious flight service between Anchorage and Seattle. He sold his controlling interest in Star Airways to David Strandberg in 1938. In later years, Dunkle regretted having sold Star Airways, which subsequently merged with other small carriers to become Alaska Airlines.

After Dunkle crashed his Travel Air on takeoff from Lake Spenard, he became involved in efforts to improve the Anchorage seaplane base. Lake Spenard was too small for larger planes to take off with cargo, so pilots had to land in Cook Inlet to pick up passengers and freight at the "Rock Pile." If the tide was out, pilots and mechanics had to piggyback passengers from Bootleggers Cove over hundreds of yards of sticky, dangerous mud flats. Two sites for float-plane base expansion were under consideration in 1934—Lake Spenard and Chester Creek. City surveyor Anton Anderson and some civic leaders without much aviation experience wanted to dam Chester Creek, which would bring the float-plane base closer to Merrill Field. Dunkle, who advocated connecting Lake Spenard by a canal to Lake Hood to provide a longer seaway, prevailed but was unable to obtain federal funds. Lobbying the territorial legislature was more effective. In June 1940, the Alaska Road Commission constructed a 100-by-2,000-foot canal, 8 feet deep, to provide a 6100-foot seaway between Spenard and Hood Lakes.

Dunkle resigned as manager of the Lucky Shot Mine in 1938 and devoted his efforts to development of the Golden Zone Mine in the Broad Pass area along the Alaska Railroad. He obtained both equipment and skilled labor from the Kennecott Mine, which ceased operation in 1938. In 1939, he reported hitting a load and shipped a bulk sample to Tacoma, where it was reported to be relatively high grade. The venture was not commercially successful because good workers began to leave to participate in prewar construction in Anchorage. No significant operation was possible during World War II, but the Army maintained one of the mine camps and a P-40 used the Dunkle airstrip until the Fairbanks airfield was completed.

Dunkle continued to fly while developing Golden Zone. He maintained airstrips on both sides of Mount McKinley, commuting frequently through Anderson Pass and surviving several forced landings. Dunkle landed float- and ski-equipped aircraft on mud flats, swamps, and soft tundra, as well as on water and snow fields. He had advantages not shared by many Alaska pilots—he knew Alaska and its weather well from his long hikes and mushes and could read maps and terrain.

The Golden Zone Mine remained inactive because of the fixed price of gold and inflation after World War II, so Dunkle opened a coal mine. On a trip in October 1957 to search for a water supply for the coal plant, the seventy-year-old mining engineer died alone on the trail, apparently from a heart attack. ■

The Era of an Autocratic Railroad Boss

Colonel Otto Ohlson took over as general manager of the Alaska Railroad in 1928. Fifty-eight-year-old Ohlson was a quick-tempered, energetic man, who was always referred to as "Colonel" because he had directed military railroads in France during World War I. He started his career as a telegraph operator in his native Sweden and later worked in South America, India, and the United States, where he rose to be head of the Lake Superior Division of the Northern Pacific Railroad.

President Calvin Coolidge, while on a Lake Superior fishing trip, was impressed by Ohlson's conscientious and determined manner and suggested that he might be a good choice to manage the Alaska Railroad. The railroad was running a $100,000 monthly deficit and was already under Congressional review. Investigators advocated austere measures: abandonment of some track, decreased traffic on the rails, increased passenger and freight rates, and strict attention to economy and business efficiency. Ohlson agreed with their recommendations and set about to run the railroad profitably, which brought him into conflict with Alaskan business leaders, who believed that the railroad had been built to promote Alaskan development rather than to make money for the government.

Ohlson's personal management style was autocratic and flamboyant. Although short and portly, he dressed in flashy clothes and was always impeccably groomed; he usually had a large Havana Partagas cigar in his mouth. Ohlson traveled up and down the railroad tracks at an excessive speed in a DeSoto sedan equipped with special rubber flanges to keep the wheels on the rails. Nothing escaped his attention, and his workers learned to both fear and respect him. Investigators sent to Alaska by the new Democratic administration in 1933 reported favorably on Ohlson's management and retained him even though he was a Republican. Ohlson accorded Interior Secretary Harold Ickes the same loyalty that he had given his superiors in the Coolidge and Hoover administrations.

Throughout the 1930s, Ohlson fought competition from trucks, buses, boats, and airplanes, and the measures he employed to stifle these

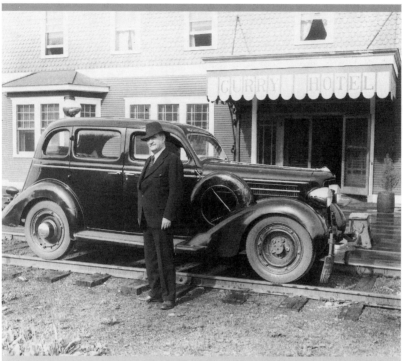

Anchorage Museum of History and Art

Colonel Otto Ohlson was notorious for speeding along the Alaska Railroad in his gas-powered DeSoto with special rail gripping attachments. The Curry Hotel (background) was where passengers spent a night when traveling between Anchorage and Fairbanks.

threats to the railroad antagonized Alaskan entrepreneurs. As road travel became more prevalent in Alaska, truckers, using the Richardson Highway from Valdez, could deliver fresh produce to Fairbanks faster than the railroad running from Seward. Secretary Ickes, who also controlled the Alaska Road Commission, restricted improvements to the highway, and Ohlson lowered railroad rates in the summer when the highway was open to make the railroad more competitive. When these measures failed to halt the truckers, Ohlson imposed a toll on trucks using the government ferry to cross the Tanana River at McCarty. Truckers countered by transporting cargo across the river on their own boats, and eventually by commandeering the ferry. The government lost the resulting court case in

Fairbanks because the jury favored the truckers. Delegate to Congress Anthony J. Dimond, who came from Valdez, fought the toll and unsuccessfully advocated for Ohlson's removal. On the other hand, Ernest Gruening, the director of the Division of Territories and Island Possessions and later governor of Alaska, stood up for Ohlson, who was his close friend and a regular bridge partner in Washington, D.C. Gruening agreed with Ickes and Ohlson that the federal government was justified in taking measures to thwart competition with its own railroad.

Ohlson also faced competition in his own backyard from motor vessels. The railroad's main competitor was Heinie Berger, who ran a passenger and freight boat service for communities on the shores of Cook Inlet. Local merchants encouraged Berger to ship directly from Seattle to Anchorage. Ohlson, who controlled the railroad's ocean dock, imposed wharfage fees that Berger refused to pay. Ohlson then barricaded the dock and punished Anchorage businesses that patronized Berger by refusing them favorable treatment on the railroad.

Competition with the developing air transport industry, a form of transportation ideally suited to Alaska's geography, was even harder for the railroad to combat. All Ohlson could do was attempt to harass these competitors, whose services continued to get better as planes became more dependable and airfields improved. Only bad weather prevented planes from becoming serious threats in all seasons.

Although Ohlson fought development that competed with the railroad, he actively encouraged colonization that would increase railroad business. Shortly after arriving in Alaska, he had the Interior Department distribute a pamphlet explaining the agricultural possibilities in Alaska and pointing out its similarities to Scandinavian countries. In 1930, the agricultural experimental station staff published *Alaska, the Newest Homeland*, an enlarged and illustrated version of Ohlson's pamphlet, and distributed it in agricultural states. Ohlson further negotiated with steamship lines to offer special rates to potential settlers. By 1931, about 110 colonists had moved to Alaska, but some only remained for a year or two.

When Jacob Baker, assistant administrator of the Federal Emergency

Rehabilitation Administration, came to Alaska in the summer of 1934 to inspect emergency public works and relief projects in the territory, a group of Anchorage businessmen took him to the Matanuska Valley. Baker returned to Anchorage enthusiastic about possibilities for agricultural settlement there. Col. Ohlson agreed to send him ideas on colonization, emphasizing the benefits of the Matanuska Valley and the advisability of choosing Northern European settlers who were used to a severe climate. Ohlson continued to push the plan by also sending copies of his memorandum to Secretary of Commerce Roper and Secretary of Interior Ickes and printing a new edition of the railroad's settlement brochure.

Ohlson went to Washington, D.C. to help the Department of Interior and FERA plan the Matanuska colony and stayed to help with preparations. When the first group of colonists arrived in Anchorage on May 20, 1935, Mayor Oscar Gill introduced Ohlson as "the father of the great movement which has brought you here." Ohlson's speech was listened to carefully by both settlers and Anchorage residents—as railroad manager, his word was practically the law of the land. He walked through the coaches shaking colonists' hands as the train sped to the Matanuska Valley. Upon arrival at Palmer, he held the box of paper slips from which the men drew their forty-acre tracts.

Ohlson continued to be one of the most active members of the board of the Alaska Rural Relocation Commission that managed the colony. Although he was frequently the target of colonists' attacks on the ARRC, Ohlson looked out for the needs of the newcomers. When a scarlet fever epidemic broke out shortly after the colonists' arrival in Palmer, he sent Dr. C. Earl Albrecht, the newly-arrived assistant to railroad physician Dr. J.H. Romig, on a special train in the middle of the night to take over medical care for the colony. Dr. Albrecht continued to practice in Palmer until he joined the Army and took charge of the hospital at the new military base in Anchorage.

Although Col. Ohlson was well beyond retirement age, he continued to serve as railroad manager and president of the ARRC board until he resigned in 1945 at the age of seventy-five. When the United States entered World War II after the bombing of Pearl Harbor in 1941, the Army was pleased to find the Alaska Railroad well-equipped and operating efficiently. Competition with other forms of transport and the minor irritations of the thirties were inconsequential under the pressures of military mobilization. During the war, Ohlson completed his greatest triumph—the Whittier cut-off, which shortened the rail distance from an ice-free port to Anchorage and bypassed the arduous railroad line from Seward. The cut-off, opened in 1943, went from the new port of Whittier on Passage Canal, an arm of Prince William Sound, across 14.2 miles and through two tunnels to Portage at the head of Turnagain Arm. Ohlson had long dreamed of such a cut-off. The Army's enthusiasm for the shortened rail line swept aside opposition from Seward. Ohlson hoped to abandon the line between Seward and Turnagain Arm after World War II, but Ickes insisted that it be rehabilitated for civilian use. The Whittier cut-off was restricted for military use.

By the end of 1945, Ohlson was exhausted. His last years of duty were unhappy because of declining mutual respect between the railroad and other federal agencies in Alaska and diminishing service to civilian consumers. In October 1945, Ohlson, now an embittered old man, lost his temper during a labor meeting and rushed across the room to shove and choke the train dispatchers' representative. A new general manager took over in 1946, and Col. Ohlson retired to Virginia, where he died in 1956. ■

6

War Effort Energizes City

Anchorage Museum of History and Art

World War II brought thousands of men to the Anchorage area. Military housing wasn't ready and many spent their first months in tents and other temporary quarters.

After two decades in the doldrums, World War II military construction jump-started Anchorage economically. Construction of airfields throughout Alaska and the Alaska Highway and Glenn Highway made

Anchorage the transportation hub of Alaska. After the war ended, military construction continued because of Alaska's pivotal position in a possible confrontation with the Soviet Union. Some veterans, who had been stationed in Alaska, returned to the Anchorage area after the war. Others came north for adventure, for construction jobs, or to take advantage of relaxed homesteading requirements. By 1950, 30,060 people, including military, lived in the Anchorage area, many of them in the burgeoning suburbs. The increased population prompted politicians and developers to demand statehood for Alaska.

In the winter of 1939-1940 the military buildup in Alaska was underway with the construction of three large naval bases, dozens of new airstrips, a cold-weather flight laboratory in Fairbanks, and a major air base and army post in Anchorage. Military planners chose Anchorage as the major operational base because of its strategic location for protection of the southern Alaska coast and Aleutian Islands. The site chosen for the Anchorage base was north of Ship Creek about four miles from downtown. Some of the 50,000 acres withdrawn for military purposes in 1939 had already been homesteaded, so the War Department purchased land and buildings from the owners. According to the Army, this location was chosen for the air base due to favorable topography and weather conditions, accessibility to the Alaska Railroad, and proximity to Cook Inlet.

In June 1940, Congress appropriated money for the Anchorage base. The first troops arrived by train from Seward on June 27. Even before the troops arrived, the Army opened a personnel office in Anchorage to hire prospective construction workers for the new base. Since the ninety cents an hour pay was excellent at the time, men from the Pacific Northwest and all parts of Alaska headed for Anchorage to sign up. Mildred Mantle, who arrived in Anchorage in March 1941, described her first impressions: "It's like a dusty Montana town with distant snow-covered mountains east and west alongside a dirty gray inlet. A sleepy little town of about 3,500 people, just beginning to stir as military construction at Fort Richardson gets underway. Just one short paved street—Fourth Avenue. Our cabin at Fifth and Gambell is way out of town. The town's main structures are the Federal Building, Providence Hospital and a modern Anchorage Hotel." The population of Anchorage more than doubled from about 4,000 in 1940 to 9,000 a year-and-a-half later.

The population boom created an immediate housing shortage. Construction workers walked the streets at night and many spread blankets and slept on the ground. Families remodeled garages or built tar-paper shacks on the back of their lots and rented them at fantastic prices. Jean Jackson, who arrived in Anchorage in April 1941, described the "house" her husband, George, built for her: "It was approximately 12 by 15 feet.... There was a potbellied stove, a sink with a pump that had to be primed, a two-burner hot plate and a Nesco oven. The bath was a galvanized tub and he had built an outhouse with a chain-pull light and it had linoleum on the floor. The so-called breakfast nook had our bedroom over it and our clothes closet was beside the breakfast nook. It had one window and one door with no key. He even had made a ladder to access the bed."

Life in Anchorage changed dramatically after the bombing of Pearl Harbor on December 7, 1941. Fearing that Alaska would be the next target, General Simon Bolivar Buckner Jr. ordered blackouts. Teacher Leah Peterson remembers, "Throughout the city a rigid blackout schedule was in effect. All windows had to have dark shades and be sealed with tape so that no light could escape. Block wardens patrolled the area to see there were no violations. All of Anchorage was to remain blacked out. There were no street lights and automobile lights were a 'no-no.' Those were dark and short winter days!" An Anchorage unit of the Alaska Territorial Guard was organized and all wives and children of military personnel, as well as newly-arrived families, were evacuated. Longtime residents were allowed to remain in town, but many of them also chose to leave. Japanese men, even those who were original Anchorage settlers, were forced to leave for internment camps.

In addition to the construction of Fort Richardson, named for General Wilds P. Richardson, the first head of the Alaska Road Commission, other large projects were built as part of war mobilization. The Army Corps of Engineers supervised the construction of the Whittier cutoff to provide the Anchorage base with a safer link to a deep-water port than the long, vulnerable railroad route from Seward. When the two long tunnels through the Kenai Peninsula mountains were completed in No-

Colonel Otto Ohlson of the Alaska Railroad and Army General Simon Bolivar Buckner commemorate the completion of the Whittier tunnel connecting the railroad to Whittier.

vember 1942, General Buckner and Colonel B.B. Talley of the Corps joined Colonel Otto Ohlson of the Alaska Railroad and engineer Anton Anderson in the "Holing Through Ceremony."

Military necessity demanded that Anchorage be connected by road with the rest of Alaska's highway system. The only road north of Anchorage was the fifty-mile spur to Palmer, and Alaska's only trunk highway was the Richardson Highway from Valdez to Fairbanks. The Alaska Road Commission started work on the 150-mile Glenn Highway from Palmer to the Richardson Highway in the spring of 1941. When the road was opened to military traffic in October 1942, Anchorage was finally on Alaska's road map. The following month, completion of the pioneer Alaska Highway through Canada meant that Anchorage was tenuously connected to the rest of the United States.

As early as 1928 an Alaskan engineer, Donald MacDonald, had mapped a practical highway route to connect Alaska to the rest of the United States. Both Alaska's Delegate to Congress Anthony J. Dimond and Alaska Governor Ernest Gruening had pushed for development of the highway, but it took the bombing of Pearl Harbor to make the government give it serious consideration. Near the end of January 1942, Gruening precipitated action on the Alaska Highway project on a trip to Washington.

On February 2, Brigadier General Clarence L. Sturdevant, Assistant to the Chief of the U.S. Army Engineers, learned the decision to build a military highway had been made and the job was his. Within days, Sturdevant's 10,000 men were building as much as eighteen miles of pioneer road each day. After years of controversy over the choice of routes, the Alaska Highway was mapped to follow a series of river valleys to connect with airstrips constructed along the route used to ferry airplanes to Russia. The Alaska Highway, completed in just eight months and eleven days, was 1,671 miles long and cost $130 million.

The bombing of Dutch Harbor and capture of Attu and Kiska Islands in the Aleutians greatly increased military action in Anchorage. The decision to retake Attu and Kiska and secure the Aleutians, with staging bases at Adak and Attu to support a possible invasion of Japan, had an electrifying effect on Anchorage. An avalanche of men and equipment poured in. The war was the biggest boom Alaska ever experienced, bigger than any of the gold rushes. Between 1941 and 1945 the American government spent over $1.5 billion in Alaska.

After the Aleutians were secured, military activities sharply declined. The 152,000 members of the armed forces in Alaska in 1943 declined to 60,000 by 1945 and to a mere 19,000 in 1946. Trouble with the Communist bloc saved Alaska from economic collapse. The territory's strategic position as the northwestern outpost of the United States and the "free world" meant thousands of servicemen and hundreds of millions of dollars would come to Alaska for an indefinite period of time. Construc-

Anchorage Museum of History and Art

A World War II field kitchen prepares meals for troops sent north to defend Alaska.

tion of a permanent Army post at Fort Richardson and a permanent Air Force base at Elmendorf started soon after World War II ended.

World War II brought the changes in Alaska that Delegate Anthony J. Dimond had unsuccessfully fought for during his early years in Washington, D.C. Realizing that the war effort would result in a population boom in Alaska, Dimond intensified his efforts to prepare the way for eventual statehood. In April 1943, he persuaded Senators William Langer of North Dakota and Patrick McCarran of Nevada to introduce an Alaska statehood bill. The following December, he submitted his own companion bill in the House. Dimond did not anticipate that action on the statehood bills would come until after the war, but he wanted to open discussion of the concept both in Congress and in Alaska. In December 1943, he distributed a document entitled *Statehood for Alaska* presenting his arguments for statehood and his conviction that Alaska was "on the threshold of a great and far-reaching development" as the result of the war, which projected Alaska "forward economically a distance that would scarcely have been achieved in twenty-five years of uninterrupted peace-time development."

In the opening paragraph he stated his democratic philosophy: "Unless we are willing to abandon our historic position, we are bound to demand statehood at the earliest practicable time. The whole form and fabric of our free government is based upon the assumption that people can govern themselves in better fashion than they can be governed by anyone else."

With the question of statehood in the hands of Congress and the people of Alaska, Dimond, who was sixty-three years old, announced his retirement to become federal judge for the Third Judicial District. After the Valdez courthouse burned in early 1940, the Third Division court was moved to the new Federal Building in Anchorage. Both Dimond and Governor Gruening endorsed their protégé E.L. (Bob) Bartlett to succeed Dimond as delegate.

Bartlett continued to push for statehood in Washington, and Alaskans heeded Dimond's plea that they commit themselves to achieving statehood. The 1945 territorial legislature passed a bill authorizing a statehood referendum, which passed in 1946 on a vote of 9,630 in favor and 6,822 opposed. The most enthusiastic support for statehood came from the Third Judicial District. Four years later, the legislature created the Alaska Statehood Committee, consisting of eleven members, selected on a nonpartisan basis by the governor and confirmed by the legislature. Robert Atwood, editor of the *Anchorage Daily Times*, was named chairman. Dimond, Bartlett, and Gruening were designated as ex-officio members of the committee, which worked to publicize the statehood issue.

In the expectation that many veterans wanted to come to Alaska and settle on the land after the war, the Department of Agriculture, in 1945, published a realistic appraisal of agricultural opportunities in Alaska. Warnings about the difficulties to be faced by settlers actually sounded like invitations to adventure to some. Governor Gruening urged, "Go North, Young Man," expecting that veterans would want to try the new frontier. "They've been places and seen things. The home town will seem too small, too set in its ways. They'll want more freedom, greater opportunities to make careers for themselves."

The Anchorage area grew a significant portion of its food in the days after World War II. A harvest crew gathers the 1947 potato crop on a Sand Lake homestead for the local market.

In 1947, Congress passed Public Law 82, which permitted veterans with at least ninety days service to substitute up to two years of their military service to satisfy homestead residence and cultivation requirements. A number of homesteads in the Anchorage area were acquired under this law, which allowed a veteran to gain title to homestead land within a year. Servicemen still in uniform could prove up on homesteads within commuting distance of the base. Some homesteaders continued working construction during the week, returning to their homesteads to join families on weekends. As soon as they had title to their land, homesteaders could sell land to developers, like Colonel M.R. (Muktuk) Marston, or subdivide the land themselves. Many current roads in the Anchorage area: Tudor, Boniface, Muldoon, Peterkin, and Kleven, were named for the original homesteaders.

The original town site of Anchorage was too small to accommodate the influx of new residents and a series of additions started with the South Addition in 1945. Areas on the outskirts of town, like Spenard, were completely unplanned. Streets in Spenard acquired names quickly, but the houses were not numbered. There were no sewers and no running water except from private wells. Electricity was only available to those who paid the city the entire cost of running lines from town and installing them. There was no police or fire protection. Stray dogs were everywhere.

The difficulty and cost connected with obtaining city electricity motivated a group of Spenard citizens to form a rural electrification cooperative. The Chugach Electric Association, an REA cooperative, was established August 20, 1947 to provide easily obtainable power to outlying areas. The REA officials were reluctant to lend money directly to CEA because it was not a governmental agency, so the Spenard Utility District was organized in May 1948 to serve as an intermediary.

Other areas on the outskirts of Anchorage also attracted new settlers. Some homesteads in the Chugiak-Eagle River, Sand Lake, and Hillside areas were actually farmed for potatoes or used to raise poultry and pigs. In 1945 Reese and Grace Tatro filed on a 130-acre tract that included Mirror Lake and established Quanta La Goose Farm, which supplied Anchorage with goslings, chicken eggs, and fryers. At the end of the decade, 995 acres were removed from the military reservation and offered as 5-acre tracts to World War II veterans.

Some new settlers came to Anchorage by boat or plane, but others drove the Alaska Highway, which was opened to civilian traffic in 1947. Jerry Hill, who had worked on the Alaska Highway in 1942 and 1943, was eager to return and put down permanent roots in Alaska. His wife Marian described their trip back to Alaska over the highway. "The Alaska Highway, over which we drove in a Jeep with a house trailer attached, seemed to me not too different from the days when Jerry worked on it. It was dusty, muddy, rocky, steep, rutty, and plain terrible. We encountered hairpin curves which we conquered in stages by driving into them part way, then backing up and attacking them from different angles. Many times we had to get out of the car and carefully examine the section of road up ahead to check whether it was safe to keep going. No matter how good a driver you were you got stuck. At one point a big Caterpillar tractor was stationed to pull motorists out of the muck one by one, us included. I'll never forget the times when we both clung anxiously to our door handles ready to bail out instantly if we started tumbling down a canyon or deep ditch. We had to be ferried across the Beach River because the highway bridge was yet to be built. The awful road, the curves, the flat tires, the anxiety of wondering whether the gas would last to the next source of supply made the trip exciting, adventurous, interesting, and even dangerous. But the marvelous scenic panoramas that opened up at virtually every turn more than made up for the difficulties we encountered. Forest fires and heavy rains blocked the road to Fairbanks, so we made Anchorage our destination instead."

In spite of the rigors of Anchorage life in the immediate post-World War II era, residents had new opportunities to enjoy amenities with the completion of projects like Cap Lathrop's Fourth Avenue Theater, which opened on Saturday, May 31, 1947 with a showing of *The Jolson Story*. Robert Atwood expressed the impact of the ornate new theater in an *Anchorage Daily Times* editorial: "The significance is one that will touch the daily lives and thinking of all persons who call Anchorage home. The Fourth Avenue theater is more than an expensive and elaborate building. It is a landmark in the development of a city in which families live, work, play and die.... Captain Lathrop, by investing his money in the Fourth Avenue theater, has shown his conviction that Anchorage has a brilliant future and his business is more than a 'boom' proposition. Other businessmen will adopt the same policy and great improvements in business and recreational facilities can be expected." ■

Fate of the Japanese Sourdoughs

"All persons of Japanese race of greater than half blood and all males of the Japanese race over 16 years of age of half blood shall be excluded from the area (Alaska) and transported to the continental limits of the United States." This proclamation issued by General Simon Bolivar Buckner Jr., on April 7, 1942, removed from Alaska more than 145 persons of Japanese origin, 121 of whom were American-born citizens of the United States.

The proclamation meant that Lieutenant John Hellenthal, the young lawyer assigned as hearing officer for the relocation of Alaska's Japanese residents, would be forced to order the incarceration of friends he had grown up with in Anchorage. "We knew it was wrong, but there wasn't anything we could do about it," Hellenthal recalled. "I told them that some of the old men would not survive the evacuation, but they wouldn't make any exceptions." Hellenthal was right. James Minano, who had arrived on Alaska's northern shore before the turn of the century as a cook on a whaling ship, died before reaching Fort Lewis, Washington. Minano, whose children and grandchildren lived in Anchorage, had been cooking at the Curry Hotel on the Alaska Railroad.

Hellenthal, who was particularly reluctant to incarcerate his friend, George Kimura, pleaded for several hours delay in making the evacuation announcement so the local draft board could draft George at an emergency meeting. George, who had attended school in Japan for several years, later served as a military interpreter in Australia and New Guinea.

The Kimura family had participated in the building of Anchorage since its founding as a railroad construction camp in 1915. Harry Kimura was a young man in Nagasaki, Japan, when President Theodore Roosevelt's Great White Fleet visited that city in 1906. The battleships and destroyers were circling the globe in an attempt to impress the world with the strength of the United States Navy. A cook on one of the battleships was too sick to continue, so Kimura was hired as a replacement for the rest of the cruise.

When the fleet returned to San Francisco, Roosevelt gave Kimura permission to remain in the United States. His life in the new country had a shaky start when he lost all his personal possessions in the 1906 San Francisco earthquake. The Southern Pacific Railroad hired him as a construction-camp cook, and he worked in the southwestern states for several years before a friend suggested that he move to Seattle. Kimura started a restaurant in Seattle and was soon prosperous enough to send to Japan for a mail-order bride, Katsuyo Yamasaki. Frank and George Kimura were born in Seattle before the depressed economy forced their father to explore business opportunities associated with railroad construction in Alaska.

The young Kimura family landed at the tent city on the banks of Ship Creek in 1915 and settled in a Fourth Avenue log cabin. Kimura started a restaurant and a bathhouse to serve construction workers. When railroad construction stalled during World War I, Kimura could not support his growing family in the United States. He sent the children, including baby William, to Japan to live with relatives until 1926, when they returned . Kimura started a tailor shop, the H.K. Hand Laundry and the Chop Suey House. The children, including Sam, who was born after his family returned to Alaska, attended school in Anchorage and helped their parents in the family businesses.

Harry Kimura was interned as an enemy alien shortly after World War II started, but his family continued running the businesses until the 1942 order to intern American-born Japanese. William, who was attending art school in Los Angeles, joined the family in an assembly center at Puyallup, Washington. "We were surrounded by barbed wire," William recalled. "They told us that the machine guns were for our protection, but they were pointed inward." Frank and his wife were expecting twins when the family was sent to the internment, but living conditions were not good, and the twins did not survive. William married Minnie Mitamura while both were interned. Minnie's father settled in Alaska in the early twentieth century and had owned a laundry in Cordova.

After about a year, Harry Kimura was released from the camp in Santa Fe, New Mexico, and allowed to join his family in Idaho. The Kimuras obtained a permit to work outside the camp under supervision and leased a small farm for the duration of the war. Their Anchorage businesses suffered from lack of supervision for four years, but the family was able to start them again when they returned to Anchorage after the war.

William continued his art career and became one of Alaska's leading artists. Sam developed his talent for photography and taught for years at the University of Alaska in Anchorage. ■

Young Stowaway Turned Glacier Pilot

When Robert Campbell Reeve arrived in Valdez in 1932, the thirty-year-old stowaway had less than a dollar in his pocket, but he had years of flying experience in South America. After repairing an Eaglerock plane belonging to Ford dealer Owen Meals, he started flying prospectors and their supplies to gold mines around Valdez— sometimes requiring glacier landings.

Reeve watched Bill Egan, an air-minded high school student, make his first solo flight. He signed the young man up as a "bombardier" to drop supplies at mining camps, and later employed Egan as his mechanic. In the summer of 1934, Bradford Washburn used Reeve as pilot for his Harvard-Dartmouth mapping expedition in the St. Elias mountains. For the next two years, using Fairchild 51 and 71 aircraft, Reeve continued bush flying, including glacier and mud-flat takeoffs and landings on skis and wheels.

After a hangar fire in 1939, Reeve was temporarily without a plane and lost out when the Civil Aeronautics Board allotted territories to fledgling air services. The military build-up prior to World War II came just in time for Reeve, who spent the next several years in Fairbanks, flying workers and supplies for construction of airstrips at Northway, Big Delta, Tanacross, Galena, Moses Point, and Nome.

Reeve moved to Anchorage in November 1942 to fly in the Aleutians under an exclusive contract with the Alaska Communications System. He spent three years during the war flying a Boeing 80-A and a Fairchild 79 through violent storms, dense fog, and high winds to the new bomber runways at Port Heiden, Cold Bay, Dutch Harbor, Umnak, Adak, and Amchitka.

After the war, all the Alaska territory except the Aleutians had been allotted to other pilots, so Reeve filed an application with the CAA to operate scheduled service on the 1,783-mile route from Anchorage to Attu. He converted an army surplus C-47 to commercial use as a DC-3 and then purchased more DC-3s. By the end of 1946, Reeve Consolidated Airways was operating two round-trip flights a week. When the military deactivated airfields at Dutch Harbor, Umnak, Port Heiden, and Cold Bay, Reeve assumed the expense of maintaining and operating them. The CAA took over operation of the Cold Bay airport after it became the main military and commercial refueling stop on flights to Asia.

In 1952, Reeve entered the territorial political arena, running a close race for delegate to Congress against the incumbent, E.L.(Bob) Bartlett. In spite of nationwide Republican victories, Bartlett, a Democrat, prevailed in Alaska. Reeve and his wife, Tillie, continued to be active Republicans.

Business continued to boom for Reeve Aleutian Airways during the Cold War while the United States Air Force was constructing Distant Early Warning sites at Port Heiden, Port Moller, Cold Bay, Cape Sarichef, Driftwood Bay, and Nikolski. In the spring of 1978, after forty-six years of active leadership, Reeve appointed his eldest son, Richard D. Reeves, President and Chief Executive Officer of Reeve Aleutian Airways, Inc. The elder Reeve died on August 25, 1980 at the age of seventy-eight. ∎

The Silver Stallion of Alaska

Colonel Simon Bolivar Buckner Jr. arrived in Anchorage on July 22, 1940 to assume command of the newly created Alaska Defense Force. Prior to his selection to command Army forces in Alaska, Col. Buckner had served two tours of duty at West Point as an instructor and commandant of cadets. He attended the Army Command and General Staff School for two years, staying on for an additional three years as an instructor, and graduated from the Army War College with honors. Buckner was very articulate, but his lack of tact had hampered his advancement in the Army. At the age of fifty-four, after thirty-three years as an Army officer, this was his first command. Lieutenant General John L. DeWitt, who was responsible for the defense of the western United States and the Territory of Alaska, had decided that the aggressive, outdoor-inclined Buckner was the ideal man for Alaska.

Buckner faced an overwhelming task. Alaska had no airfields fit for military aircraft and no surface connection with the rest of the United States. Alaska's sole Army installation was the Chilkoot Barracks at Haines, which had not changed in the forty years since it had been built to guard the gold trail to the Klondike. Governor Ernest Gruening described: "Chilkoot Barracks had about as much relevance to modern warfare as one of those frontier-fighting posts from the days of Custer and Sitting Bull. It had no road or air connection with the outside world. Its only transportation was provided by a fifty-one-year-old harbor tug. When we went up the Lynn Canal, the terminal fjord of the Inside Passage, we encountered a thirty knot head wind that stopped us cold and stranded us for three days. We had to be rescued by the Coast Guard. If war had come we'd have had to sue for peace and ask for a wind-check."

Initially Buckner operated with limited funding; he used the time to travel extensively and learn his territory. When not traveling, he spent his first Alaska winter living in a tent on the site of Elmendorf airfield to be near his men. He bathed in an outdoor tub each morn-

General Simon Bolivar Buckner meets local royalty at the 1941 Coronation Balls.

ing after his orderly removed ice with a blow torch. On August 31, he pinned on the stars of a brigadier general and celebrated by going duck hunting with the two English setters he brought with him from Kentucky. He protested that servicemen were not eligible for resident hunting licenses. When the Alaska Game Commission refused him a resident license, he took the case to court.

After his men moved into their barracks, Buckner rented a house in Anchorage, sent for his family, and began entertaining his new Anchorage friends. His personal popularity went far toward opening Anchorage homes to military personnel. This example of fraternizing with civilians helped Anchorage prepare for its new role as Alaska's military metropolis.

When Congress voted a $350-million defense construction budget including $12.8 million for Alaska, Buckner's work began in earnest. During the fall of 1940, hordes of construction workers arrived at Alaskan ports. They were hardly off their boats when Buckner had them at work. At Anchorage, he was building Elmendorf Air Base and Fort Richardson, which was to be his headquarters. In addition, he built Ladd Field at Fairbanks and smaller airfields, antiaircraft sites, and ground troop posts throughout Alaska. When necessary he used Army troops to work shoulder-to-shoulder with civilian workers. With miraculous speed, miles of runway were hewn out of the tundra, scores of barracks raised, and hundreds of gun emplacements scooped out. Buckner received a steadily increasing amount of equipment, which presented a problem because there were so few roads in Alaska. To avoid pile-ups of equipment on the docks, he hired bush pilots to haul supplies to the new air fields. Communications were also a problem. When General DeWitt ordered a July Fourth alert from Point Barrow to Panama, the word took four days to reach all stations in Alaska.

When the United States entered the war after the bombing of Pearl Harbor on December 7, 1941, Alaskan defenses had been significantly improved since Buckner's arrival eighteen months before. In fighting the war he had to share command with the Navy. In June 1942, after the bombing of Dutch Harbor and the capture of Attu and Kiska, he complained he was not being consulted on operations. Admiral Theobald at Kodiak was not as eager to attack the Japanese as Buckner. Generals Buckner and DeWitt pressed the Joint Chiefs for authority to move out on the Aleutian Chain and to establish bases within striking distance of the Japanese. Adak, 250 miles from Kiska and more than 350 miles from the advance American base on Umnak, was finally chosen for the Aleutian base. Troops moved in on August 30.

Buckner had established the Alaska Scouts, a small commando unit consisting of Alaskan Natives and seasoned outdoorsmen under the command of Colonel Lawrence V. Castner. The Alaska Scouts trained in the Anchorage area before their service in the Aleutians. Without lights or sound, Castner and thirty-seven commandos landed on Kuluk Bay and found Adak Island had not been occupied by Japanese. Buckner sent his senior engineer, Colonel Benjamin B. Talley, who had already built the Cold Bay and Umnak air fields, to Adak to join the landing force. In less than two weeks, Adak was ready for war. The United States had pushed its front line 400 miles closer to Japan. Next the Scouts slipped onto Amchitka Island and assessed the possibility of establishing an air field there.

In the meantime, Buckner's Alaska Defense Command reached the size and stature of a combat army of 150,000. As the military preparations continued in the Aleutians, operations shifted to the Navy's Alaska Sector Building at the Kodiak Naval Base.

After the Aleutian Campaign, Buckner assumed total military control of the Alaska-Aleutian region, including all Air Force operations. However, his big job had become a small one and soon he moved on. In June 1944, he went to Hawaii to organize the new Tenth Army for the final Pacific offensive against Japan. Buckner's postwar plans were set—he planned to retire and live in Anchorage on a bluff overlooking Knik Arm. These plans never materialized . On Easter morning in 1945, Lieutenant General Buckner landed on the beach in Okinawa. On the eve of victory in June, he went to a forward observation post and was fatally wounded by shrapnel from a Japanese artillery shell. ■

"Muktuk" Marston: a Man of Vision

Marvin R. Marston was one of the foresighted men who came to Alaska during World War II, saw the potential for development in the Anchorage area, and stayed to capitalize on it during the postwar years. Marston was born before the turn of the century in Tyler, Washington and grew up in Seattle. He briefly worked in Nome, before attending college in Illinois. After speculating in oil and real estate in California, he spent thirteen years prospecting and mining in the open bush country of Northern Ontario and Quebec. When Canada entered World War II, he found his financial assets frozen and went to Washington, D.C. to propose a plan for underground storage of airplanes.

The Pentagon wasn't interested in Marston's proposal, but decided to take advantage of his knowledge of northern terrain and weather conditions. In March 1941 he accepted a major's commission and embarked for Anchorage, where he was assigned as morale officer for Elmendorf Air Force base. He developed recreational opportunitie. With a crew of dedicated outdoorsmen, he scouted the surrounding mountains for the best location for a ski development and settled on an open slope valley high in the Chugach Mountains behind town. The Army erected the first rope tows at the Arctic Valley ski area, which has served both military and civilian skiers in Anchorage for over fifty years.

Marston also recognized the value of a service club for enlisted men. A total of 628 men worked to build the log "Kashim," which was dedicated in March 1942 at a wild game barbecue with comedian Joe E. Brown as a special guest. Brown entertained troops throughout Alaska and set an example for other Hollywood celebrities who made morale-raising visits. Marston used a B-17 and crew to take Brown to every military outpost in the territory and logged over 9,000 miles in less than a month. During this tour Marston discovered Western Alaska lacked defenses against a feared Japanese invasion. He realized that placing a massive army along the western fringe of the territory was not feasible, but he felt the Native people who knew how to survive in the Arctic could be organized into an efficient guerrilla army. He presented his plan to General Buckner, but received little support until the Japanese bombed Dutch Harbor in June 1942. Governor Ernest Gruening joined forces with Marston. Gruening, who was

Colonel "Muktuk" Marston enjoyed the outdoor life of Alaska.

already organizing citizen militias in the major cities, recognized Marston as a
kindred spirit and was delighted to have the Air Force major help him organize
the Alaska Territorial Guard.

Gruening and Marston flew to Bristol Bay and along the coast to the Arctic villages in the summer of 1942. Marston's standard speech ended, "We will give you guns and ammunition. If the Japanese comes [sic] here and lands [sic] his boat will you shoot him quick? You men who will help your country against the Japanese, come forward now and sign your names here on this paper." Native men signed up by the thousands as Eskimo Scouts in nearly every Arctic village Marston and Gruening could reach by boat, airplane, or dog team. During these village trips, Marston acquired the nickname "Muktuk" as a result of an eating contest in which he outlasted a native chief in devouring raw whale blubber. Governor Gruening advanced Marston's cause and even argued with General Buckner about a promotion for the major.

Marston resigned from the Air Corps after World War II. Although he continued his interest in the Alaska Territorial Guard following the war, he directed his main efforts toward civilian development in the Anchorage area. His family, which had been evacuated during the war, returned. Along with other investors, including Walter J. Hickel, Marston purchased two homesteads covering the area between Cook Inlet and Northern Lights Blvd. (then known as KFQD Road) from Fish Creek to Clay Products Road. The McCollie homestead had been staked by a dentist in 1936 and the Lyn Ary homestead by a Russian immigrant, who had been a supply sergeant in the Russian army.

The Marston family spread their fishing nets on the beach, planted potatoes, and enjoyed entertaining visitors from all over Alaska at cookouts on the homesteads. They sold portions of land to local residents who built some of Anchorage's finest homes on the bluffs overlooking Fish Creek and Cook Inlet. In 1952, Marston and Ken Kadow built Anchorage's first suburban subdivision, Turnagain by the Sea, with a water system and paved streets to serve 150 homes. In spite of a temporary setback when a portion of his property was destroyed in the 1964 earthquake, Marston's real estate developments have thrived and have continued to be operated by Muktuk's son Brooke.

Marston was active in the statehood movement and was elected a delegate to the Constitutional Convention in 1955. During deliberations, he was a strong advocate for Native rights, presenting a floor amendment to grant land to Alaska Natives. He tried to convince the Resource Committee to include such grants in

Anchorage of the 1940s was a small place, but after World War II it experienced explosive growth as many families moved north looking for a new future.

their draft article. However, this group deferred to the federal government in the area of Native rights. Subsequent statehood bills required Alaska to disclaim all rights to property of Alaska Natives in favor of the federal government, but Marston did not agree that a disclaimer was sufficient to meet the state's obligations to Alaska's original inhabitants.

Muktuk never forgot the loyal soldiers of the Arctic who served him so well during World War II. He maintained contact with Native leaders and appealed to Alaskans to include Natives as equal partners in building the state. In 1973, the State of Alaska gave Marston the rank the regular military refused to grant him, designating him a Brigadier General in the Alaska National Guard. After his death on July 21, 1980, at the age of ninety, former Governor Bill Egan referred to him as "a human dynamo who dared to disturb the status quo." ∎

7

The Battle for Statehood

In 1952 contractors were building suburbs around the city.

United States involvement in the Korean War and the Cold War during the 1950s assured the military would continue to play a major role in Anchorage's development. In October 1950, a new Fort Richardson opened in the Chugach foothills north of the original post. Elmendorf Field was turned over to the Air Force and became the home of the Alaskan Air Command. Civilian aviation boomed with hundreds of new bush airfields, electronic devices to make flying safer, a new International Airport, and an influx of international carriers flying to all parts of the world. In addition to construction workers and military personnel, a group of young, professionally-trained veterans headed north to take advantage of opportunities in the growing city. Anchorage, meanwhile, was striving to provide services for the new people who were accustomed to urban housing, utilities, and schools. The new Alaskans resented territorial status and enthusiastically joined the statehood movement. The fortuitous discovery of oil on the Kenai Peninsula south of Anchorage in 1957 finally convinced Congress that Alaska could afford statehood. In January 1959 Alaska was admitted to the Union as the 49th state.

World War II increased awareness of Alaska's strategic role in any future conflicts. While memories of the war in the Pacific were still fresh, the United States military realized the need to protect America's back door. The Union of Soviet Socialist Republics became increasingly expansionist. By 1950 its domination of Eastern Europe was complete. "Iron Curtain" became the term symbolizing a malevolent force and watchwords of the day were containment and balance of power. Alaska had many installations in place from the military World War II buildup, although some had been deactivated. Following a visit to Alaskan military bases in 1947 by General Dwight D. Eisenhower, the United States began a major rebuilding of Alaskan Air Command facilities.

One of the AAC's first goals was construction of a permanent Aircraft Control and Warning system. The existing air defense system was improved and a new radar system developed. By 1952, defense sites at Cape Lisburne, Cape Newenham, Cape Romanzof, Tin City, Northeast Cape, Campion, Tatalina, King Salmon, Indian Mountain, Sparrevohn, Murphy Dome, and Fire Island (near Anchorage) were operational.

Construction on the Distant Early Warning System began in 1952 with the first "trial balloon" finished at Barter Island. Subsequently, thirty-four White Alice installations successfully linked AC&W and DEW line sites into a cohesive network that could relay communications to Elmendorf in Anchorage and Eielson Air Force Base in Fairbanks. ("Alice" was the acronym for Alaska Integrated Communications Enterprise. Since code names required two words, "White" was selected because it seemed appropriate for Alaskan winters. Alice White was the name of a silent-movie actress so the two words were transposed.)

Additional construction in the Anchorage area started in 1955 when the military decided to place Nike Hercules missile systems at selected sites near Anchorage and Fairbanks to defend its major installations and the local populations. The three sites near Anchorage were Site Summit in the Chugach Mountains overlooking the town, Site Point at Campbell Point on Turnagain Arm, and Site Bay at Goose Bay across Knik Arm. Site Summit was a challenge to build due to steep terrain and harsh climate. Workers blasted rocky ridges to cut roads and provide a level site for the battery control area. Operation of a Nike battery involved 125 people who staffed the site twenty-four hours a day.

With the construction of Fort Richardson as a permanent army post, several recreational facilities became available to the civilian population under certain restrictions. Civilians could play golf at the new Moose Run Golf Course as long as they were invited guests of active military, retired military, or civilian employees of military establishments. The staff of the new Alaska Native Medical Center in Anchorage, which was taken over by the United States Public Health Service in 1955, also enjoyed military privileges at commissaries and recreational facilities. When rope tows on the military side of the Arctic Valley Ski Area became too crowded in the early 1950s, Anchorage Ski Club members erected tows of their own farther up the valley. However, skiers still relied on the military for maintenance and snow removal on the road, which also provided access to Site Summit.

In 1946, the Civil Aeronautics Board selected Anchorage as the North American terminal on the Great Circle route joining the United States with Tokyo, Seoul, Shanghai, and Manila. After the new Anchorage International Airport was inaugurated on December 10, 1951, international air carriers began filing applications for landing rights. Scandinavian Airlines filed in 1954, followed by Air France and KLM Royal Dutch Airlines in 1958, and Japan Airlines in 1959. Anchorage became the first Ameri-

Float planes line the shore of Lake Hood adjacent to Anchorage International Airport.

can city to have nonstop passenger airline service to both Europe and Asia.

In the early 1950s Anchorage had two paved streets, a stoplight on Fourth Avenue, two small skyscraper apartments, and a new high school. In spite of spending nearly $5 million to improve city utilities and streets and another $1.6 million to build schools, Anchorage was still having a difficult time keeping up with the influx of people. To provide additional power for the downtown area the *Sacketts Harbor*, a salvaged oil tanker with a 5,400-kilowatt generator, was beached at the port until improvements could be made at the Eklutna power plant. Even so, power outages frequently occurred. Most available housing was substandard. Since there were no building codes outside city limits, tar-paper shacks and trailers constituted much of the housing.

In the early fifties the City of Anchorage included only the original town site and the South Addition, a twenty-one-block area annexed in

1945. The city population in 1950 was 11,250, with an additional 18,800 people living outside the city on homesteads and in suburbs like Spenard, Eastchester, Mountain View, and Woodland Park. Haphazard subdivisions were springing up, connected by gravel roads and dirt trails. Recognizing the problems of dealing with such a population boom, the National Municipal League and *Look* magazine named Anchorage an "All-American City" in 1956 for "successfully tackling a skyrocketing population that threatened to swamp city facilities and pushing for needed civic improvements."

Annexation became a political issue. Some areas resisted because they didn't want city services or felt they couldn't afford the taxes. Since voters repeatedly turned down imposition of a sales tax, property owners had to carry the burden. Owners of bars, strip joints, and massage parlors didn't want to be under city jurisdiction, but their neighbors agitated for annexation. In 1954, four sections of Eastchester were annexed. Russian Jack Springs, deeded to the city by the military in 1958, was annexed, as was Rogers Park, a ten-square-mile area with only about 450 people. Annexations of Spenard and most of Fairview in 1959 increased the city population to 37,000 in a 12.7-mile area.

Most accessible parts of the Anchorage bowl had already been homesteaded by 1950, when completion of the Seward Highway made additional land in the Chugach foothills south of Anchorage reachable by motor vehicle. Phyllis and Leroy Allinger, Frances and David Prator, and the Elmore family homesteaded in the Rabbit Creek area in 1950. About that time the Land Office opened an area of five-acre home sites near a jeep trail that connected the Seward Highway and Campbell Airstrip. Since a petition to improve this trail was placed in the office of Dr. James O'Malley, the trail became known as O'Malley Road. Dr. O'Malley was not one of the original homesteaders, but he did own a five-acre tract in the area for a short time.

Although statehood for Alaska seemed to be imminent under the Truman administration, President Eisenhower was reluctant to endorse it when he became president in 1952. Since the Democratic party had been strong in Alaska under Delegates Dimond and Bartlett and Governor Gruening, the Republican administration in Washington assumed that Alaska would send Democrats to Congress. When Republican Senator Hugh Butler of Nebraska, an arch statehood foe, announced that he was bringing a group of senators to Alaska to listen to the "little men" who could not afford to travel to Washington, a group of Anchorage residents formed the "Little Men for Statehood." They took charge of welcoming the senators and organizing testimony. This group, subsequently, changed its name to Operation Statehood. In 1954, Operation Statehood organized a group of statehood supporters to fly to Washington, D.C., at their own expense in order to lobby President Eisenhower at the same time that a delegation from Hawaii was in the capital city.

This effort failed to sway the Republican administration, so the 1955 Alaska Territorial Legislature passed legislation establishing a convention to draft a constitution for the potential new state as evidence that Alaska was prepared for statehood. A special election was held on September 13 to choose fifty-five delegates to the Constitutional Convention. The delegates elected from Anchorage included: Dorothy J. Awes, a lawyer active in the League of Women Voters; Seaborn J. Buckalew, a young lawyer who had served in the 1955 legislature; Edward V. Davis, a lawyer and member of the Anchorage School Board; Helen Fisher, Secretary of Operation Statehood; Victor Fischer, Planning Director for the City of Anchorage; John S. Hellenthal, a lawyer and member of the Greater Anchorage Health District Board; Herbert H. Hilscher, president of the Cook Inlet Historical Society; Steve McCutcheon, photographer and former territorial legislator; George M. McLaughlin, Anchorage city magistrate; Marvin R. Marston, organizer of the Native Alaskan Guard; Chris Poulsen, a former Anchorage city councilman; Victor C. Rivers, a member of the Alaska Statehood Committee; and Barrie M. White, president of Operation Statehood.

The Constitutional Convention began its work in November 1955 at the University of Alaska campus in Fairbanks and completed deliberations on February 6, 1956. During its session, the Convention listened to George Lehleitner, a New Orleans businessman who had espoused the cause of statehood for Hawaii and Alaska, argue for adoption of the Tennessee Plan, whereby a prospective state would

After Congress approved Statehood for Alaska in 1958, Miss Alaska Rita Martin, the future wife of U.S. Senator Mike Gravel, attached a 49th star to a giant U.S. flag draped over the side of the old Federal Building in downtown Anchorage.

elect delegations to Congress in advance of actually being seated and rely on these prospective senators and representatives to serve as on-site lobbyists for statehood. The concept was endorsed by the Convention as the Alaska-Tennessee Plan.

In the April 1956 regular primary election, Alaskans voted to endorse the Constitution and two additional ordinances—one abolishing fish traps and the other accepting the Alaska-Tennessee Plan. Ernest Gruening and William A. Egan, who had been chairman of the Constitutional Convention, were elected as "senators," and Ralph Rivers as "representative." The three men spent part of 1957 and 1958 in Washington, D.C., and were present on May 28, 1958 when the Alaska Statehood Bill passed in the House of Representatives on a vote of 208 to 166 and on June 30 when the Senate concurred on a

109

vote of 64 to 20. Upon receipt of this news, the *Anchorage Daily Times* put out an extra edition with the seven-inch headline "WE'RE IN." The city celebrated with a huge bonfire on the Park Strip. The President signed the bill on July 7, and, on August 26, Alaskans voted 40,452 to 8,010 for the immediate admission of Alaska to the Union.

Although many people, both in Alaska and in Washington, D.C., played important roles in expediting statehood, the factor that may have tipped the scales was the discovery of oil on the Kenai Peninsula south of Anchorage in 1957. Prior to this indication of a bright financial future for Alaska, Congress questioned the northern territory's ability to assume the costs of statehood.

Geologists had predicted for decades that oil would be found in Alaska because of oil seepages in several areas, but wells drilled on the Alaska Peninsula and near Katalla on the Gulf of Alaska had been disappointing. Troubling events in international oil fields during the early 1950s prompted major oil companies to again start looking for petroleum in Alaska. When the Eisenhower administration took office in 1952, Secretary of the Interior Douglas McKay released large areas of previously closed federal lands for oil exploration. A deluge of oil lease applications flooded the Anchorage Bureau of Land Management office. Oil companies were restricted in the number of leases they could file on; consequently they encouraged others to file so they could acquire leases from them. Since the filing fee was only twenty-five cents an acre and leases could be resold to oil companies for a dollar an acre, filing on oil leases became a booming business in Anchorage. Jack Roderick established a scouting service and published bulletins containing the names of oil men coming into the state and information on where they were interested in exploring. Locke Jacobs, an enterprising clerk at the local Army-Navy Store, studied oil geology and the intricacies of the Land Office operation and became the conduit through which Anchorage businessmen speculated on oil leases.

A group of prominent Anchorage residents, which included Robert B. Atwood, *Anchorage Daily Times* publisher, and his brother-in-law Elmer Rasmuson, head of the National Bank of Alaska, worked with Jacobs to acquire oil leases in various areas including the Kenai National Moose Range, which Interior Secretary McKay opened for oil exploration. These businessmen were so anxious to promote Alaska development that they offered a block of leases free to any company that would actually drill a well on their leased land. The large oil companies were not interested in their offer, but one small company, Richfield Oil, decided to drill a well in Alaska.

A Richfield geologist who studied U.S. Geological Survey maps discovered a promising area on the Kenai Peninsula and the company leased 70,000 surrounding acres. In March 1955, Richfield sent geologist William Bishop to Alaska with instructions to find oil. Bishop located a promising oil-bearing structure which extended into the property that the Anchorage businessmen had leased through Jacobs. The businessmen were glad to sell leases on 60,000 acres adjoining the Richfield leases for twenty-five cents an acre with an override should Richfield strike oil.

Bishop persuaded Richfield's president, Charles S. Jones, to expedite drilling at the Swanson River site twenty-three miles from the nearest road. He reportedly marked a road to the site by stringing toilet paper from a low-flying Piper Cub. Then he twisted his boot heel in the snow, and posted a sign saying "drill here." Richfield started drilling in April 1957 and struck oil on July 15. Alaska was on its way to becoming an oil-rich state and a group of Anchorage businessmen were on their way to becoming multi-millionaires. Bishop's bronzed boots are on display at the Anchorage Museum of History and Art. ∎

Darkness at Noon

A group of tourists traveling by train from Seward to Anchorage on the morning of July 9, 1953 experienced a phenomenon that wasn't mentioned in their travel folders. When they left the SS *Aleutian* in Seward that morning, the day was bright and sunny. At about 11:30 a.m. they saw a weird-looking purple cloud in the northeast with a very clear line of demarcation between it and the blue sky. As they got closer to the cloud, the sky darkened. Some of the tourists feared the cloud came from an atomic bomb explosion or a tornado. When the train stopped in Anchorage, lights in the cars went out and some passengers became hysterical. The conductor left to make a telephone call and returned with his clothes coated with

Anchorage Museum of History and Art

Ash from the eruption of Mt. Spurr darkened the skies of Anchorage in the summer of 1953. Along 4th Avenue Anchorage drivers needed headlights and city street lights to see.

ash. He explained that Mt. Spurr, a volcano eighty miles west of Anchorage, had erupted and poured ash on the city.

Anchorage street lights automatically turned on at 11 a.m., indicating visibility of less than fifty feet. Fearing a power outage, the city turned the lights off. The Civil Aeronautics Administration at Kenai reported three eruptions from different locations on Mt. Spurr, timed at 8:55, 10:55, and 11 a.m. Military and private pilots hurried to land, fearing that the sulfurous content of the ash would damage metal on their aircraft.

Mt. Spurr and Mt. Trident, 380 miles southwest of Anchorage, continued to steam for several days while residents shoveled heavy bucketfuls of debris. Ash removed from a ten-by-seven-foot sidewalk in front of the Reeve Aleutian Airways office weighed thirty-five pounds.

Although the 1953 eruptions were the most dramatic in recent history, the volcanoes near Anchorage are among the most active in the world. Mt. Redoubt across Cook Inlet from Kenai erupted several times during the next thirty years and Mt. Augustine south of Homer dusted Anchorage with enough ash to interfere with skiing one winter. Mt. Spurr behaved itself for thirty-nine years. In August 1992, Spurr erupted again, dumping enough ash on Anchorage to suspend air travel. Airlines have avoided volcanic eruptions since a KLM airliner suffered severe damage from flying through an ash cloud when Redoubt erupted in December 1989. ■

Irene Ryan—Right Woman at the Right Time

Irene Irvine, a twenty-one-year-old woman looking for adventure, first came to Alaska in 1931. The Depression was at its height and there were no jobs at home in Texas. Working as a waitress at the Anchorage Grill and as a bank teller, she earned enough money to take flying lessons at Merrill Field; she became the first woman in Alaska to earn a private pilot's license. Looking back on her early days in Alaska, she recalled, "I came from an oil family in Texas and you develop a feel about oil. I saw oil discovered by dowsers who waved a willow branch over a map and by people who just had a hunch, but I had faith that, with emerging technology, major oil deposits could be found in Alaska in a scientific way. I flew over the state border to border in 1931-32 and marveled at the potential. I felt people should be looking for oil instead of gold. Everyone thought I was nuts."

Irene left Alaska to gain the scientific basis necessary to search for oil. She was the first woman to graduate from the New Mexico School of Mines with a bachelor of science degree in geological engineering. In 1941, she returned to Anchorage with her contractor husband, John Edward "Pat" Ryan, and one-year-old daughter, Marcella. Mrs. Ryan practiced as a civil, mining, geological, and petroleum engineer for both federal agencies and private engineering firms. Among her many professional projects were design of Anchorage International Airport and sixteen other major Alaska airports, construction of the military pipeline from Skagway through Canada to Fairbanks, design and construction of housing subdivisions in Anchorage, and development of geologic maps and surveys for Anchorage Gas and Oil Development, Inc. Both Ryans were active in the fight for statehood as members of Operation Statehood.

When dealing in oil leases became a major economic enterprise in the Anchorage area in the 1950s, Irene Ryan was the only local person who had knowledge about petroleum geology and the federal leasing system. Locke Jacobs, the Army-Navy Surplus store clerk who became Anchorage's predominant lease broker, obtained his first oil and gas map of Southcentral from Irene Ryan. She organized her own leasing group, which included some of her Democratic colleagues. She acquired some potentially valuable leases but oil was not actually discovered on any of them.

Mrs. Ryan's greatest contribution to Alaska was the influence that she had on the politicians who had to make important policy decisions regarding the state's dealings with major oil companies. She served in the 1955 and 1957 Alaska Territorial House of Representatives and was responsible for convincing the governor that Alaska needed a conservation law like that in Texas so landowners competing for oil in a field would be compelled to coordinate drilling. Thanks to the foresight of Irene Ryan, Alaskans could collect the benefits when oil started to flow. She kept her colleagues in the territorial legislature in extended session until they passed an oil tax during the oil lease activity in 1955. She insisted on a one percent levy on the gross value at the well of all oil and gas produced in Alaska.

When Bill Egan became the state's first governor in 1959, he relied on State Senator Ryan for advice regarding oil and gas policy. Upon her recommendation, he appointed Phil Holdsworth to be his first Commissioner of Natural Resources. Egan selected Irene Ryan as his Commissioner of Economic Development during his final term as governor in 1970. She received an honorary doctor of science degree from Alaska Pacific University in 1985 and was named Alaskan of the Year in 1986. Irene Ryan died in Anchorage on November 23, 1997 at the age of eighty-eight. ■

The Atwoods of Anchorage

Anchorage Daily Times Editor Robert Bruce Atwood and his wife Evangeline worked as a team to orchestrate Anchorage growth during the 1940s and 1950s. Unwilling to merely report contemporary happenings, Bob Atwood enthusiastically promoted the future he foresaw for his hometown, engaging in political and business issues while Evangeline spearheaded Anchorage's cultural development. She described their partnership: "Bob and I have a different approach to these community problems, but it's not a male-female approach. I've had time to do research which has helped him work out his ideas because he was busy running a newspaper. He was busy making history and I was busy recording it. I never worried about being eclipsed by my husband, but always worked shoulder to shoulder with him."

Anchorage Museum of History and Art

Bill Lofflen presents Bob Atwood a Conn cornet replacement at his newspaper office.

The Atwoods met and married in Illinois, where Evangeline worked as a social worker and Bob as a court reporter for the *State Journal* in Springfield. They returned to Worcester, Massachusetts, Bob's home town, and were both working as reporters for the *Worcester Telegram* when Evangeline's father, Edward Anton Rasmuson, president of the National Bank of Alaska, wrote that the *Anchorage Daily Times* was for sale. Loans from his father-in-law's bank enabled Atwood to move to Anchorage and buy the paper in 1935. Bob described his activities as a small-town newspaper editor: "Here I had this little paper that should have been a weekly, but it had big city responsibilities. Everyone was looking for news of the territory and the world. We worked day and night trying to do it....I had to spend the morning putting the paper out and the afternoon selling ads, and the evening writing editorials." Atwood relied on bush pilots for news of rural communities and provided them with papers to distribute in villages and mining camps to acquaint people with Anchorage businesses. As a result, the pilots brought so much business to town that airlines had to hire help to fill the orders.

Atwood often joked that he was forced to promote Anchorage development because Evangeline had no intention of staying married to a small-town publisher. At times he used innovative measures to produce results. Atwood was a member of the Greeting Committee when Postmaster General James Farley came to Alaska to visit the new Matanuska Valley colonization project. Upon returning to Anchorage, Atwood suggested that it would be appropriate for the postmaster general to break ground for the new federal building. Farley consented and posed with a shovel of dirt in a potato patch on Fourth Avenue. When Farley asked about the status of funding for the federal building, Atwood admitted that there wasn't any yet, but that Anchorage was hoping it would be forthcoming. Funding was promptly approved for the new concrete federal building to house the post office and other federal offices. The Third Division Court moved from Valdez to the new Anchorage federal building after the Valdez courthouse burned in 1940.

Atwood's next big job was to get the military to commit to a major long-term operation in Anchorage. During a news famine in 1936 he published an article listing twenty-two reasons for locating an air base near Anchorage and sent copies to the War Department in Washington, D.C. The 1940 construction of the original Fort Richardson was a gift that kept on giving as far as Anchorage is concerned. Evangeline and Bob entertained the high-ranking officers assigned to local bases and made sure the Anchorage community accepted military personnel with open arms. In later years Bob reminisced, "I don't know where else in the world I could have lived and had the experiences I had here. It's a privileged life to know all the generals and the people that run the military that come through here."

After World War II, Atwood promoted the building of Anchorage International Airport and helped persuade international carriers to base there for great circle flights to the Orient and trans-polar flights to Europe. During the next three decades Anchorage advertised itself as the Air Crossroads of the World. To popularize the new Alyeska ski area in the 1960s, the *Times* sponsored International Airline ski races that lured skiers from Europe and Asia to compete and enjoy a grand party.

Whenever the federal government was planning to spend dollars, build structures, or create agencies in Alaska, Atwood wanted them located in Anchorage. To make sure that a new Alaska Native Health Service hospital was built in Anchorage instead of Palmer in 1953, Atwood persuaded Mayor Zachary Loussac to offer any building site the federal officials wanted even if it might mean moving City Hall.

The Atwoods' primary cause during the 1950s was statehood for Alaska. Bob headed the Alaska Statehood Committee for twelve years and Evangeline founded the Alaska Statehood Association, which established branches in communities throughout the territory to popularize the statehood issue and enlist celebrities throughout the United States in the cause. Evangeline's first book, *83 Years of Neglect*, published in 1950, and the 1957 publication of *Anchorage, All-American City* helped energize the statehood movement. Bob's only venture into politics came in 1956 when he ran for Tennessee Plan senator against William A. Egan. Atwood underestimated the ability and popularity of the young Valdez grocer who had chaired the Constitutional Convention and was stunned by his defeat. A lifelong Republican, Atwood was one of the Alaska leaders present when President Eisenhower signed the Alaska Statehood Act on June 25, 1958.

While Anchorage was growing and struggling with local government issues, Evangeline was making sure that citizen organizations were in place to influence development. She formed the Anchorage Parent-Teacher Council over the objections of a superintendent of schools who didn't want parents interfering in the way he ran the schools. She also started the Alaska Federation of Women's Clubs and served as its president for two terms. She founded the League of Women Voters in 1950 and the Cook Inlet Historical Society. In 1958, Evangeline started the World Affairs Council and served for more than six years as its executive director. She also supported the arts and helped to found the Anchorage Community Theater and the Anchorage Opera Association.

Evangeline continued to be active in a variety of community activities and published several additional books: *We Shall Be Remembered*, a history of the Matanuska colony; *Who's Who In Alaska Politics*, with Robert DeArmond; *Frontier Politics; Alaska's James Wickersham*; and *Anchorage Star of the North*. She received an honorary doctor of literature degree from the University of Alaska Fairbanks in 1967 and was awarded a doctor of humane letters degree from Alaska Pacific University in 1982.

Anchorage Museum of History and Art

Evangeline Atwood was a historian and advocate of arts in the community.

Along with the rest of Anchorage, the Atwoods suffered a setback in 1964, when their log home was destroyed in the earthquake. Bob was at home practicing on his trumpet when the quake hit. He watched his house break up and fall into a chasm. He couldn't pull his arm free and realized that he was still holding on to the trumpet, which was buried in the sand. The *Times* rallied frightened Anchorage residents, urging people to rebuild bigger and better than before. The Atwoods provided an example by building a columned showplace residence, on the edge of the earthquake disaster area.

When oil executives began arriving in Anchorage in the 1960s, the Atwoods welcomed them as enthusiastically as they had the military brass to make sure that Anchorage would become corporate headquarters for the oil industry. Anchorage was acquiring such a large share of Alaska's new development that other communities began to get envious of the "new kid on the block." Anchorage had already taken Cordova's railroad, Valdez's courthouse, the Native hospital that Palmer wanted, and was threatening the Fairbanks university with a new Anchorage campus. The *Anchorage Daily Times* promotion for moving the capital from Juneau was the last straw. The capital move proposition failed twice in statewide elections before it passed in 1974 with the stipulation that a new capital city be created in the Railbelt area no closer than 80 miles from Anchorage or Fairbanks. After a lengthy process of deciding upon a site for the new capital city, Juneau succeeded in persuading voters to turn down bonds necessary for funding the move in 1982. During the decades that Bob Atwood was pushing the capital move, the *Anchorage Daily Times* was condemned in Juneau.

For more than forty years, Atwood ran a profitable newspaper and acquired a personal fortune from investment in oil leases. However, even his millions were not enough to save the *Times* when new owners of the rival *Anchorage Daily News* challenged him in a newspaper war. Kay Fanning had kept the struggling *News* alive for years by investing her own money. In 1979 she approached C.K. McClatchy, head of a California newspaper chain, and he persuaded his board of directors to buy an eighty percent interest in the *News*. During the next decade, Anchorage residents enjoyed both a conservative and a liberal editorial voice, but eventually the *News* prevailed. Afternoon papers like the *Times* suffered everywhere as their readers came to rely on television news reports. Atwood saw the end coming and sold the *Times* in 1989 to Bill Allen, owner of an oil field service company that had just made millions in the *Exxon Valdez* oil spill cleanup. The *Times* stopped publication in 1992.

Evangeline Atwood died in Anchorage on November 5, 1987 and Robert Atwood died at the age of eighty-nine on January 10, 1997. Anchorage has numerous reminders of the generosity of the Atwoods. The largest theater in the Performing Arts Center is named for Evangeline, and the Alaska Pacific University building where the Alaska Native Land Claims Settlement Act was signed was renamed the Atwood Center in 1983. The Atwood Foundation also sponsors a visiting professorship in journalism at the University of Alaska, Anchorage. ◼

Augie Hiebert—Eyes and Ears of Alaska

August Hiebert was a fifteen-year-old farm boy in central Washington state when he acquired his ham radio license in April 1932. A small shed behind the farmhouse with a single boxed-in bed and a potbelly stove became the home of W7CBF, which Augie put together from cannibalized parts. Rather than working in the family orchards, young Hiebert enrolled in an electronics correspondence school and landed his first job at station KPQ in Wenatchee, Washington.

Anchorage Museum of History and Art

Augie Heibert was known as a hands on manager.

In the fall of 1938, Augie went to work for Stan Bennett, the chief engineer at KBND in Bend, Oregon. When Bennett left to help Cap Lathrop establish KFAR in Fairbanks, he asked Hiebert to help him. Augie arrived in Fairbanks on August 23, 1939 and helped complete the transmitter installation. His first job was to build rhombic antennas to pick up shortwave news.

Hiebert and Bennett "bached" in the one-room apartment at the transmitter building and tuned in shortwave bands when they were not copying war news. Austin Cooley, Cap Lathrop's inventor nephew, who was working on developing facsimile technology, had an experimental license to transmit fax over a 1,000-watt amateur radio unit. Cooley tested his invention each Sunday morning by transmitting pictures from his equipment in New York City to Hiebert and Bennett at the KFAR transmitter building in Fairbanks.

On Sunday morning, December 7, 1941, when Hiebert was anticipating a transmission from Cooley, he became the first person in Alaska to hear of the attack on Pearl Harbor. He alerted the commanding officer at Ladd Field, who relayed the news to General Buckner in Anchorage. Wartime regulations put an end to the experiments with facsimile transmission at KFAR, but General "Hap" Arnold learned of Cooley's invention and worked with him to develop a means for transmitting weather maps from Russia. Hiebert's petition for a commission in the Signal Corps was rejected because his contributions as a civilian radio engineer were considered vital to the war effort.

After the war, Cap Lathrop decided that the time was right to locate a station in Anchorage. He sent Hiebert to Anchorage in July 1947 as technical director to build the KENI transmitter at a handsome art-deco building located in a wooded area overlooking the mouth of Chester Creek. The KENI studios and offices were located in the new Lathrop Building, which housed the Fourth Avenue Theater. Two years later, Hiebert became KENI-AM manager.

After his mentor and financial backer, Cap Lathrop, died in a 1950 accident at the Healy coal mine, Hiebert tried to persuade the Lathrop estate executors to start a television station. "My feeling at the time was that we should go into television," Hiebert argued. "In those days one of the problems we had was that Alaska was really a man's country. With no amenities, there were many family problems—you could have a marvelous employee, but with restlessness at home, it was hard to find and keep good help....The board turned me down—they felt TV would compete with radio and film."

Hiebert turned in his resignation in 1953 and started Northern Television, Inc., with $25,000 seed money left him in Cap's will. He raised additional money by selling stock to Anchorage business people. KTVA-TV, the city's first television station, started broadcasting on December 11, 1953. People in Fairbanks wanted a television station of their own, so

Northern Television answered the challenge and established KTVF-TV, which started broadcasting on February 17, 1955. Although Hiebert served the two smallest television markets in the country, he succeeded in acquiring a CBS affiliation.

Hiebert recognized FM radio was the wave of the future in the late 1950s and introduced KNIK-FM in Anchorage as the state's first FM radio station. The McKinley Building that housed both the TV and FM radio stations in Anchorage was severely damaged in the massive earthquake on Good Friday 1964. Although the plumbing pipes were broken and water soaked the transmitters, Hiebert had the station back on the air in a week's time. "We had to wear hard hats on the air," he recalled. "The building had no heat and no water. We got little oil stoves and a space heater for the big studio, and put chimneys out the side of the building."

In 1965 Northern Television acquired KBYR-AM in Anchorage and KFRB-AM in Fairbanks. The AM station in Anchorage attracted Hiebert because it was on land in Spenard that was large enough to accommo-date a 392-foot tower. A Small Business Administration disaster aid loan enabled Northern Television to place its TV station and both AM and FM radio signals on one tower and increase the TV station from 3,000 to 30,000 watts. Hiebert was still recovering from the Anchorage earth-quake when the August 1967 flood covered the entire office, studio, and TV operation in the basement of the Northward Building in downtown Fairbanks with fourteen feet of water.

Before the Fairbanks flood, Hiebert had been working with Senator E.L.(Bob) Bartlett to promote satellite communication in Alaska. The first satellite demonstration, originally scheduled for August 15, 1967 to commemorate the Alaska Purchase Centennial, was fortuitously delayed by the Six-Day War in the Middle East—Hiebert was glad not to have witnessed half-a-million dollars worth of equipment floating down the Chena River. After Senator Bartlett's death in December 1968, Hiebert counseled Bartlett's successor, Senator Ted Stevens, on Alaska telecommu-nications. Following a meeting between Secretary of Defense Melvin Laird and Senator Stevens, COMSAT's application was approved and

Alvin O. Bramstedt interviews Bob Atwood on KENI-TV.

construction of Alaska's first earth station at Talkeetna began in the spring of 1969. Hiebert received the 1969 Gold Pan Award in Anchorage for pioneering in Alaska satellite communications.

On July 21, 1969, during the initial phase of construction on the earth station, Alaska had its first taste of satellite communication. Through the energetic efforts of Alaska's congressional delegation, Secretary Laird approved the use of a military mobile ground station and satellite to bring the live lunar landing coverage to Anchorage. Anchorage welcomed people from throughout Alaska who came to view the historic event. Alaska Airlines offered reduced fares for the week of the broadcast.

The Talkeetna earth station was dedicated in honor and in memory of Senator Bartlett on June 30, 1970. Throughout the day, Hiebert coordinated satellite transmissions from Tokyo, Guam, and Hawaii for use in a composite program simulcast later that evening on competitors KENI-TV and KTVA-TV. The incoming live transmission from Tokyo carried a message to Hiebert from his daughter Peggy, who was a hostess at the Alaskan Exhibit for Expo '70 in Osaka. The outgoing satellite signals beamed blanket toss and gold panning to Japanese viewers.

On January 3, 1971, Anchorage residents watching KTVA saw their first live telecast from outside Alaska—a National Football Conference championship game between the Dallas Cowboys and the San Francisco 49ers and in color. The first live satellite television transmission originating in Alaska to the Lower 48—the Department of Interior's Environmental Impact Hearings on the Trans-Alaska oil pipeline—followed shortly on February 24, 1971. The eyes of the world were on Alaska on September 26, 1971 when President Richard M. Nixon met Japan's Emperor Hirohito in Anchorage.

Television was scheduled to come via satellite to Alaska's villages for the first time in January 1977 but Rural Alaska Television Network, known as RATNET, supporters were waiting federal approval. Hiebert flew to Washington, D.C., where he found the village transmitter applications stuck in processing at the Federal Communications Commission. He explained the project would bring together the state's residents and put them in touch with the world. His argument was persuasive and a telegram authorizing the RATNET channel went out immediately. In addition to bringing rural villages on-line for television, the state decided to introduce some villages to educational television. Since it was a struggle to balance education and entertainment programming to the satisfaction of rural television viewers, the state legislature funded an additional educational transponder in 1980.

In the 1980s Northern Television undertook a massive equipment transformation and spent $3,000,000 on a new, high-power TV transmitter and antenna, a new FM transmitter with higher power, and a new FM antenna for better stereo sound. Hiebert was recognized by both the University of Alaska Fairbanks and Anchorage Community College for meritorious service during the 1980s. He served as Master of Ceremonies for the statewide live radio and television simulcast commemorating the 25th Anniversary of Statehood in 1984. Although Hiebert retired from Northern Television in May 1997 at the age of eighty-one, he continues to serve on the board of directors. ■

An Eskimo blanket toss highlights an early Fur Rendezvous in Anchorage.

8

Good Friday Earthquake

Anchorage Museum of History and Art

Downtown Anchorage suffered heavy property damage in the 1964 Good Friday earthquake, one of the most powerful quakes ever recorded in North America, which killed 115 people.

By 1960 Anchorage was well-established as headquarters for the oil industry in Alaska. Oil was starting to flow from the Swanson River field on the Kenai Peninsula and geologists were looking for more oil on the North Slope and under Cook Inlet. Military construction, however, was decreasing. The Anchorage economy had leveled off when North America's largest earthquake struck Southcentral Alaska on Good Friday 1964. Generous federal assistance and the buoyancy of local developers helped Anchorage emerge from the disaster with a booming construction industry and a functioning year-round port.

The Alaska Statehood Act provided the new 49th state with the opportunity of selecting 103 million acres of federal land. Fortunately the state selected some of its land, including a coastal tract on the North Slope, before 1966 when Secretary of the Interior Stewart Udall froze all future land selections pending resolution of aboriginal land claims. Discovery of oil on the North Slope in 1968 and a highly productive state lease sale in September 1969 persuaded oil companies to join Native peoples in an effort to resolve the land claims issue so that oil development and pipeline construction could proceed.

Population of the Anchorage area increased steadily from 82,833 in 1960 to 126,385 at the end of the decade.

By the start of the sixties, eighteen oil companies had already opened offices in Anchorage and geological survey crews were beginning to operate in Alaska. The Swanson River oil field was in full production, with fifty-two wells that supported construction of a refinery at the port of Nikiski north of Kenai. An underwater pipeline from Kenai to Anchorage brought residents more economical energy. Oil exploration moved to the west side of Cook Inlet on leases acquired at state sales of submerged lands in December 1959 and December 1961. Amoco's Chakachatna group, consisting of Sinclair, Phillips, Skelly, and Amoco, began drilling on Middle Ground Shoal on May 15, 1962. Shell began drilling five days later for a group that also included Chevron and Richfield. Although both wells produced oil, the Amoco group was awarded the discovery royalty. Lights from oil-drilling platforms across the inlet were visible in Anchorage at night.

Cook Inlet oil exploration resulted in an unexpected series of events in 1962. Three Native trappers from the village of Tyonek across the inlet from Anchorage discovered several white people with an oil-drilling rig in the middle of their ancestral hunting grounds. The drillers refused to leave; one of the village leaders contacted Stanley McCutcheon, an Anchorage lawyer who had befriended the poverty-stricken village. When McCutcheon heard about the rig, he saw an opportunity to help his Native friends because Tyonek was

Anchorage Museum of History and Art

Oil production continues year round in Cook Inlet where the oil platforms are built to withstand winter and one of the strongest tides in the world.

one of the few Alaskan villages that was located on reservation land.

In 1915, President Woodrow Wilson signed an order setting aside 24,000 acres surrounding Tyonek as the Moquawkie Reservation, which was supervised by the Bureau of Indian Affairs. Without notifying the villagers, the BIA had leased a section of the Tyonek reservation to the Pan American Oil Company and placed the money in a government fund. A swift court injunction stopped the drilling, and McCutcheon sued the Department of Interior to prevent the BIA from selling oil and

129

gas leases on the reservation without consent of the Tyonek Village Council. The village proceeded to renegotiate all oil exploration leases on its reservation, generating about $12.5 million. Tyonek Natives used their newly gained wealth to replace their hovels with modern houses, to erect an up-to-date school, and to ship tons of rice to poor villages elsewhere in Alaska.

Although the Tyonek boom was short-lived, it left an indelible mark on Anchorage and the rest of Alaska by helping Natives throughout the state organize and press their aboriginal claims on lands the state wanted to select. The Alaska Statehood Bill provided that the new state could select 103 million acres of unreserved federal land in order to give the state a means of generating revenue for running its government. Land ownership was a new concept to most Alaska Natives, but, as soon as the state started selecting land, Natives throughout Alaska saw their use of land might be restricted. When Native leaders, like Willie Hensley and Emil Notti, suggested that all Natives should get together and discuss the problem, the Tyonek Village Council agreed to pay travel and room expenses for delegates and arranged a meeting place in Anchorage. On October 6, 1966, 300 Native delegates from all parts of Alaska met in a deserted Fourth Avenue storeroom in Anchorage to form the Alaska Federation of Natives. Tyonek Natives suffered a tragic setback when their young leader, Albert Kaloa Jr., died in an Anchorage hotel fire, but they continued to pay for the services of Stanley McCutcheon and his law partner, Clifford Groh Sr., to help Native organizations become legal entities that could file land claims to block state selections in their regions.

Emil Notti, the first AFN president, created a land claims committee, which drafted a position statement contending Alaska Natives were victimized and wanted reparations. Native organizations claimed most of the land in Alaska, completely stymieing the state's selection process. Interior Secretary Udall, sensitive to the Native position and the national mood of supporting civil rights, froze all land transferal in 1966 pending resolution of the Native claims.

Land selection was only one task facing the new state in the sixties.

An escalator was a big hit at the new Northern Lights Shopping Center in April 1961.

In addition to creating a structure for state government and a judicial system, the state needed to establish mechanisms for local government. In an effort to avoid local government proliferation that plagues many metropolitan areas in the rest of the nation, framers of Alaska's constitution specifically excluded county government. Instead, they made provisions for boroughs, which they hoped could provide services where necessary without overlapping or duplicating city services.

In October 1959, Anchorage voters had approved a Home Rule Charter for the city, but a large portion of the Anchorage area remained outside city limits. Although the State Legislature enacted the Borough Act of 1961, which provided for local initiative in the formation of boroughs, the Anchorage area did not voluntarily take any action toward borough formation. The Legislature enacted the

131

Mandatory Borough Act of 1963, requiring the incorporation of boroughs effective January 1, 1964. The second-class Greater Anchorage Borough, approved by voters in December 1963, assumed area-wide powers of planning and zoning, education, property assessment, and tax collection. The second-class status required voter approval for additional powers and functions that the borough might wish to undertake. The Mandatory Borough Act allowed a transition period of two years from the time of borough incorporation for the transfer of area-wide powers and the school board to the new borough.

While this governmental transition took place, military construction projects were nearing completion. The Anchorage area was suffering from an economic slump with high unemployment when, on March 27, 1964, Southcentral Alaska experienced the strongest earthquake ever recorded in North America. The quake, initially said to register 8.4 on the Richter scale, but since upgraded to 9.2, hit at 5:36 p.m. with its epicenter 150 miles southeast of Anchorage under the waters of Prince William Sound. In addition to Anchorage, Valdez, Seward, Kodiak, and Whittier received severe quake and tidal wave damage. The tidal wave virtually destroyed the Native villages of Chenega on Prince William Sound and Old Harbor and Kaguyak on Kodiak Island. Only 115 lives were lost, most from the tidal waves. The death toll would undoubtedly have been much higher had the quake not occurred in the late afternoon on Good Friday, when schools and businesses were closed.

In Anchorage, the most populated community affected, the quake triggered three large landslides in the most built-up areas of the city. The Fourth Avenue slide damaged a large portion of the central business district, while the L Street and Turnagain slides affected two of the most valuable residential areas.

Along downtown Fourth Avenue, the ground broke in an irregular line in front of a row of buildings, which sank straight down so that the marquee of the Denali Theater, which fortunately was not occupied at the time, came to rest on the street surface. The Fourth Avenue Theater, where 700 children were watching a Disney movie, rode out the quake with very little damage. The slides and quake vibration destroyed or severely damaged about thirty blocks of dwell-

A traffic controller was killed when a tower collapsed at Anchorage International Airport.

ings and commercial buildings in downtown. Workmen had already gone home when the Four Seasons, a six-story apartment building, completed but not yet open, collapsed. The five-story J.C. Penney department store on Fifth Avenue dropped a curtain wall of precast panels to the street, killing two persons.

To the east of the Fourth Avenue slide, behind the Alaska Native Hospital, a section of bluff 120 ft. deep and 650 ft. wide fractured and moved north. Although the hospital parking lot and lawn lowered as much as twenty-five feet, the hospital sustained only minor damage. Across the flats, the shaking earth loosened clay beneath Government Hill, dropping the south wing of Government Hill Elementary School about thirty feet and collapsing the east wing.

The most devastating earth movement occurred in the Turnagain Heights subdivision, where some of the city's most prominent families were relaxing before dinner. The clay formation under the bluffs broke loose, and the ground gave way in a concave pattern

133

along 4,300 ft. of the choicest property in the subdivision. Houses, streets, trees, cars in driveways—everything on the bluff side of the breakaway—began moving toward the Knik Arm tidal flats. Family members were separated in the moving mass where clay ridges nineteen to twenty feet high emerged and crevices opened destroying about seventy-five homes, some of which rode the slide down below the former bluff level. Most residents managed to escape as their houses broke up, but three people died in the Turnagain slide.

Residential areas along the shore of Knik Arm were temporarily evacuated for fear of a tidal wave, but Anchorage was spared the fate of Seward, Kodiak, Whittier, Chenega, Old Harbor, Kaguyak, and Crescent City, California, where tidal waves caused most of the fatalities. Only seven deaths occurred in the Anchorage area: three in the downtown slide area; three in the Turnagain slide; and an air traffic controller who died when the Anchorage International Airport tower collapsed.

Anchorage had not developed a specific plan to react to a natural disaster. Most disaster planning at the time envisioned an atomic bomb attack and stored food and hospital supplies in underground shelters. However, city officials gravitated to the Public Safety Building, which had escaped serious damage and had communication facilities. At a 3 a.m. Saturday meeting, Mayor George Sharrock cited two immediate priorities—accounting for missing people and attending to health and sanitation concerns. An army rescue unit and members of the volunteer Alaska Rescue Group searched the downtown and Turnagain wreckage without finding additional casualties.

An amateur radio operator contacted Governor William Egan in Juneau to get permission to utilize the Alaska National Guard troops who were just completing a two-week encampment at Fort Richardson to patrol the damaged areas and provide emergency food, water, and sanitation equipment. Anchorage was fortunate to have a nearby military presence that was immediately available to provide manpower and services until civilian utilities could be made functional. Although aftershocks shook the entire region for days there was no panic, fire, or looting. The Alaska Railroad and the highway between Seward and Anchorage were severely damaged but air traffic was not seriously affected. Some residents left Anchorage temporarily until normal services were in place, but most displaced residents stayed in town by moving in with friends in areas where utilities still functioned. Public schools opened in a week, although some were double shifted until repairs to severely damaged schools were completed. For several weeks the surviving Natives from Kodiak Island villages were housed in Anchorage elementary schools, necessitating additional double shifting.

President Lyndon Johnson reacted immediately to Governor Egan's request that the state be declared a major disaster area and the Office of Emergency Planning gave unprecedented financial assistance to the restoration of federal, state, and local public facilities. The Alaska Omnibus Act, which had provided Alaska with increased federal assistance during the first five years of statehood, was extended. Amendments to the Omnibus Act increased the federal share of primary highway reconstruction funding from 50 percent to 94.4 percent and allowed for expansion of small boat harbors. The federal contribution to the urban renewal disaster projects was increased from 75 percent to 90 percent, and individual and business losses were compensated for by liberalizing normal disaster aid policies.

According to initial estimates of damages to public and private facilities, the Anchorage area sustained losses of over $200 million—about half of the total state losses. The greatest property damage and loss was in the public sector of the economy, most of which was federally owned and controlled or was to be restored in large part by federal funds. The burden of private reconstruction was eased by generous federal aid in the form of loans on favorable terms, forgiveness or adjustments on mortgages and other obligations, and tax adjustments. The cost of rebuilding to Alaskans was actually lower than the damage figures would suggest. The job was undertaken at a relatively rapid rate since the construction industry had suffered a continuing decline in the years prior to the earthquake and a supply of underutilized labor and other resources was readily available.

The impact on communities varied greatly. Anchorage sustained the greatest property damage but did not have as great loss of life or crippling effect on the local economy as coastal towns and villages. Valdez was wiped out and its normal economic life ended until construction on a relocated town site was completed. Seward lost its multi-million-dollar waterfront and rail terminus—its transportation-based economy was forced to suspend operations until facilities could be rebuilt. In the meantime the Port of Anchorage gained a lasting advantage in the competition for freight.

The pre-earthquake facilities at the Port of Anchorage, located at the head of Cook Inlet about a mile from downtown Anchorage, consisted of a single-berth dock and an industrial park area. The dock had been completed in 1961, but no regularly scheduled carrier used the facilities and the port operated at a loss. Shortly before the earthquake, city officials began negotiating for weekly service. Shipping companies, which preferred the ice-free ports, usually unloaded cargo at Seward or Whittier and transported freight to Anchorage and Fairbanks on the Alaska Railroad. Although the ports of Anchorage, Seward, and Whittier were all damaged in the quake, tidal waves caused the greatest damage at Seward and Whittier. Emergency repairs at Anchorage were begun immediately and the port was able to receive its first vessel in three days. In addition to the emergency shipping, which normally would have gone to one of the other ports, Anchorage began receiving oil tankers of companies that had petroleum-storage farms at Seward and Whittier. Because Anchorage was the only facility operational for some time after the disaster, several oil companies built new installations in the Anchorage industrial park.

SeaLand, the company that had been negotiating with the Port of Anchorage prior to the earthquake, began general cargo operation in May 1964. The following winter SeaLand successfully demonstrated that the Port of Anchorage could be used in the winter as well as the summer. As a result of this increased use of port facilities, which were operating for the first time without a loss, bond issues passed to enable construction of a petroleum dock and a second general cargo dock.

In retrospect, Alaska's economy benefited from the earthquake. The State of Alaska was facing a critical financial period in its political development just before the disaster. Federal transition funds and programs, designed to provide a gradual weaning from territorial dependence on the federal government, were about to end, but the quake justified an

Sealand started using the Anchorage port year-round after the 1964 Earthquake.

extension of these programs and the state treasury emerged in better shape than it would have been under normal conditions. As the largest center of government and construction in the state, the Anchorage area received the most benefit from the reconstruction activities. The Port of Anchorage permanently captured the bulk of freight movement into Southcentral and Interior Alaska from the rival ports of Seward, Whittier, and Valdez. In spite of rebuilding and improvements to its port facilities, Seward never regained the freight it lost to Anchorage following the quake. Anchorage had finally proved that it could be the transportation center of Alaska for sea as well as land and air.

Task force groups and private individuals rushed to Anchorage with advice regarding reconstruction work. They identified high risk areas and recommended that further construction in those areas be curtailed unless some form of stabilization could be undertaken. As a preventive measure against future slides, funds were made available for construction of an earth buttress to protect the downtown area. No recommendations were made for stabilization of the L Street slide area, which was classified for single-family dwellings and parks. Between 1964 and 1967, however, the city issued several permits for large building, including the Captain Cook Hotel, in the L Street slide area. By building this twelve-story luxury hotel, Walter J. Hickel demonstrated his optimism and faith in the future of Anchorage.

Several methods of stabilizing the Turnagain slide area were considered, but the city council voted against urban renewal in the area. Disregarding recommendations of consulting engineers, the city issued building permits and the Federal Housing Administration, which had suspended all financing in the slide area following the earthquake, agreed to insure loans landward to the slide scarp with the stipulation that buyers were informed that the FHA would not be responsible for losses should another earthquake occur. Some residents who lost homes in the quake retained their land and rebuilt.

Anchorage was well on the road to recovery in 1967, when the state celebrated the Alaska Purchase Centennial. A 50-member Centennial Commission planned a number of projects to commemorate Alaska's first 100 years under the American flag. Vintage trains towed carloads of residents through the railroad yards and Alaska Airlines personnel, dressed in gay nineties finery, announced that they were "setting down in Anchor Town" in Robert Service rhyme. The most lasting of the Anchorage

The historic September 10, 1969 North Slope oil lease sale brought more than $900 million to the State of Alaska and initiated twenty-five years of rapid growth.

centennial projects was the original east wing of the Anchorage Museum of History and Art. As he turned the first shovel of sod at the ground breaking ceremony, Mayor Elmer Rasmuson stated that the museum was "the biggest cultural catalyst Anchorage has ever had."

Although the Anchorage economy was looking good in 1967, the best was yet to come. On February 16, 1968, Harry Jamison, Atlantic Richfield general manager, announced a major oil discovery at Prudhoe Bay on Alaska's North Slope. The ARCO discovery prompted British Petroleum, which had just about given up drilling on the North Slope, to try again. The success of its Put River 1 well in 1969 indicated that BP would have a large share of the Prudhoe Bay oil field, which, fortuitously, was on land successfully claimed by the State of Alaska prior to the land freeze.

Anchorage, as the corporate center for Alaska oil activity, was bound to benefit from these discoveries even though Prudhoe Bay was almost a thousand miles north. Oil executives moved into town and upscale subdivisions developed to accommodate them. The state, which needed funds to continue the earthquake rehabilitation in Anchorage and to help Fairbanks recover from a debilitating flood in 1967, decided to offer more oil leases on state land near Prudhoe Bay for competitive bidding.

The September 10, 1969 oil lease sale, which was held in Anchorage's Sydney Laurence Auditorium nearly two years after the initial discovery, drew a large crowd of oil people and reporters. The biggest spender at the sale was a consortium that included Herbert and Bunker Hunt and their trusts, along with Amerada Oil, Getty Oil, Louisiana Land and Exploration Company, Marathon Oil, and Placid Oil, a Hunt subsidiary. This consortium alone paid more than $240 million for five tracts within the Prudhoe Bay structure and subsequently drilled a productive well on the land. BP succeeded in adding more acreage to its field, and ARCO leased land in four new areas of the North Slope. As a result of the sale, the State of Alaska was richer by almost a billion dollars.

The biggest problem facing the oil companies was how to transport oil from Alaska's North Slope to the other forty-nine states. An attempt to open a northwest ocean passage with the cargo-vessel *Manhattan* required the help of icebreakers and proved too expensive to be economically feasible. A pipeline was the other option. In October 1968, ARCO, Humble, and BP formed the Trans-Alaska Pipeline System (TAPS) to make pipeline feasibility studies. In 1969, additional companies joined the consortium and within months TAPS applied to the Department of Interior for permission to construct a hot-oil pipeline across nearly 800 miles from Prudhoe Bay to the port of Valdez. Since a pipeline would traverse lands claimed by Native peoples and tied up by the land freeze, the sixties ended with great expectations, but also with problems to overcome. ∎

White Elephant

The Anchorage Centennial Committee spent 1966 considering appropriate projects to commemorate the 100-year anniversary of the purchase of Alaska. Establishing a zoo was a seriously considered project. Jack Snyder, owner of S&F Foodland, discovered a contest sponsored by Chiffon Toilet Tissue. The store that sold the most toilet paper would receive the choice of $3,000 or a baby elephant. Snyder won the contest with the help of a Fairbanks grocer and chose the elephant, which he planned to donate to the Centennial Committee.

In the meantime, Anchorage voters turned down a ballot proposition to develop a zoo. When the fifteen-month-old Asian elephant arrived, the Centennial Committee had no interest in receiving Snyder's gift. Since elephants cannot stay outside during an Alaskan winter, Snyder asked Sammye Seawell, owner of the Diamond H Riding Stable, to temporarily house his "white elephant." He arrived at the stable with a thermometer and found the stall adequately warm for the 300-pound baby named Annabelle.

The stable was to be temporary until a permanent placement could be found. For a while Snyder transported Annabelle to his market each day, enticing her with apples to climb in his truck. Eventually Annabelle refused to get in the truck, so Snyder offered her permanently to Seawell. She accepted; she had become attached to the little elephant, which she had been feeding rye milk from a gallon bottle. Seawell enlisted her son-in-law, Dr. Ed Voke, and friends to help her incorporate the Anchorage Zoo in 1968. School children volunteered to raise money for Annabelle's care. Parents formed a board of directors, and the zoo opened in August 1969 with Annabelle, a seal, an arctic fox, and two black bear cubs. The zoo made an arrangement with the Alaska Fish and Game Department to house abandoned baby animals until permanent homes could be found. In the spring of 1975, Fish and Game brought in a polar bear cub that had been rescued in the Beaufort Sea. The cub, which Anchorage children named Binky, was an instant favorite and the community raised $200,000 to build a new concrete facility for him so he would not have to be sent away when he outgrew his original quarters. Binky was two-and-a-half years old when he moved into his new home—a 42-

A toilet paper sales contest brought Annabelle the elephant to Anchorage.

foot-wide play area with a heated pool holding 53,000 gallons of water.

The following year, a pair of cubs, one male and one female, joined Binky. Siku, the female, stayed in Anchorage as Binky's mate, but the male, Nuka, was donated to a Mexican zoo when he and Binky developed an animosity. Binky and Siku charmed Anchorage children until 1995, when they both died from infection. The Anchorage Zoo was without a polar bear until the spring of 1998 when Ahpun, a female cub, was brought to the zoo. A new facility for Annabelle eventually was constructed. Her radiant-heated home included a public viewing area and a quarter-acre exercise yard. Maggie, an African elephant, was purchased as a companion. Annabelle earned part of her keep painting pictures sold at the zoo gift shop. After thirty years as one of the primary attractions at the Anchorage Zoo, Annabelle died in 1998 from a foot infection.

Most of the animals at the zoo are native to Alaska, but llamas, two Bactrian camels, and three Siberian tigers give Anchorage children the opportunity to observe non-Alaskan animals. A petting zoo allows children close contact with small domestic farm animals. The zoo remains a nonprofit corporation, relying on private donations and entrance fees. Although the it gets no regular government funding, the municipal assembly and state legislature have appropriated funds for specific capital improvements. ∎

Growth of the University District

The expanding population and economy in Anchorage during the 1960s fostered the establishment of an area on the outskirts of town that could provide adequate space for new and improved public service facilities. By the end of the decade, new universities, a modern general hospital, a psychiatric hospital, and a youth correctional facility were located in the forested parklike area destined to become Anchorage's university district.

Under the leadership of Reverend Peter Gordon Gould, the Methodist Division of National Missions chose Anchorage as the site for a liberal arts four-year college. Rev. Gould, the first Alaska Native to be ordained in the Methodist clergy, grew up in the Methodist Jesse Lee Home at Unalaska and worked for years to encourage the founding of a private liberal arts college to provide access to learning for Alaskans. He wrote that "...the most significant need of Alaska is for indigenous leadership—leadership reared, educated, and trained in Alaska for Alaska." His vision was shared by a group of Anchorage citizens, who raised $700,000. The Board of National Missions matched the local contribution and purchased 300 acres of wooded land from the Bureau of Land Management for a campus. Alaska Methodist University was dedicated on June 29, 1959 and enrolled its first students in 1960.

The new university, under the leadership of President Frederick McGinnis, was a cultural center for Anchorage during the 1960s. Three major buildings were constructed during the McGinnis administration: Grant Hall, Gould Hall, and the Atwood Center, designed by world-famous architect Edward Durrell Stone. The drama department, with Frank Brink as director, produced a series of Broadway-quality plays in the Grant Hall auditorium. Banners announcing the production of the Thornton Wilder play *Our Town* were displayed all over town when the 1964 earthquake shattered Anchorage. The play went on as scheduled, providing citizens with welcome relief from the destruction around them. Cross-country ski coach Jim Mahafey built ski trails through the university campus and developed local skiers with sufficient ability to compete in the 1964 Winter Olympic Games in Japan.

Anchorage Community College, officially organized January 1, 1954, under the Community College Enabling Act, offered classes at West High School before moving to a new campus on land adjoining Alaska Methodist University in 1968. In 1976, when Anchorage Community College expanded and eventually joined the University of Alaska Anchorage, a full branch of the state university system, Alaska Methodist University closed temporarily. The next year AMU reassessed its mission and reopened as Alaska Pacific University with a new program focused on international relations. Alaska Pacific University regained accreditation, established graduate-level programs and attracted local financial support for the

Anchorage Museum of History and Art

Providence Hospital was built in the University District in the early 1960s.

construction of more buildings, including the Mlakar President's Home in 1983, Grace Hall in 1984, the Ruth and Homer Mosely Sports Center in 1986, and the Carr Gottstein Academic Center in 1992. The University of Alaska Anchorage campus also continued to expand, adding academic and business buildings, a sports complex, the Wendy Williamson Auditorium, a fine arts building, an administration building, and the Lucy Cuddy Center. The two universities share the Consortium Library.

New oil money helped Anchorage keep up with the medical needs of the expanding population. Since the thirty-year-old Providence Hospital at Ninth and L Street was no longer adequate, the Sisters of Providence erected a new modern hospital on land adjoining the university. Patients moved to the new, hospital on October 26, 1962. The new hospital, fortunately located on stable land, was functioning efficiently when the earthquake hit. The medical complex continued to grow with additional beds, physician offices, a frostbite and burn center, a cancer therapy center, and Providence House where patients and families from out of town can be housed while receiving treatment.

The 225-bed Alaska Psychiatric Hospital also opened in the university area with the first patient admitted on October 15, 1962. Prior to statehood Alaska's mentally ill and developmentally disabled residents were transported to Morningside Hospital, a private mental institution in Portland, Oregon. When the State of Alaska took responsibility for Alaska's mentally ill after statehood, mentally ill Morningside patients were brought back to this new institution in Anchorage; most of the developmentally disabled Alaskans were moved to Harborview Development Center in Valdez.

The state of Alaska also constructed the McLaughlin Youth Correctional Center in the university area. This institution, which provides both detention and long-term treatment of juvenile offenders, was established in 1968. ■

Anchorage Becomes a Destination for Skiers

During the sixties, Anchorage residents began to capitalize on long winters with consistent snow cover. Alpine skiing was becoming increasingly popular throughout the United States, and many new Alaskans were already enthusiastic skiers. In World War II the Army developed a ski area at Arctic Valley in the Chugach Mountains overlooking Anchorage, and civilian skiers added to the slopes with rope tows of their own. As Anchorage Ski Club membership grew, it was evident that three long rope tows were not sufficient to meet demand. Planning for the purchase of a T-bar started in 1959 with money raised through sale of life memberships. Volunteers excavated ground for installation of the towers and the T-bar lift, with a 984-foot vertical rise, was dedicated on December 15, 1960—a day when the temperature registered twenty degrees below zero. In 1969 the rope tow that rose 813 vertical feet was replaced with a double chair lift.

While Ski Club members were enjoying the new T-bar, a more ambitious ski development was underway near Girdwood, the old mining town on Turnagain Arm thirty miles south of town. Alaskan ski buffs Bob Bursiel, Sven Johanssen, and Ernie Bauman, who explored the area by helicopter and light plane, recognized Mt. Alyeska could be one of the best mountains anywhere for skiing. They hired Frances Richins Clark of Anchorage to find investors interested in financing ski lift construction. She located Francois "Frenchy" deGunsburg, an oil-lease broker for Onawah Oil Company. He convinced his company to invest in the first phase of development, which included a Pomalift, clearing of ski trails, and construction of a small lodge and manager's living quarters. The first chair lift and day lodge were built in 1960, but the small local market was not sufficient to make the development profitable for several years.

Although deGunsburg and Onawah had to subsidize Alyeska during the early years, in time the resort was discovered by foreign skiers, who were employees of airlines using Anchorage as a refueling base. *Anchorage*

Daily Times editor Robert Atwood recognized Alyeska's appeal to airline personnel as an asset and promoted Alyeska as the site for International Airlines Ski Races. In 1967 deGunsberg decided to sell the resort and entered into a three-year management contract with Alaska Airlines with an option to purchase. Chris von Imhof, director of tourism for the State of Alaska, who had skied at Alyeska and was impressed with its potential, agreed to be general manager. Construction of a seventy-five room hotel and condominium units were completed prior to 1970.

As Alyeska became more popular, additional chair lifts opened higher slopes with more reliable snow cover. Both winter and summer use of the area increased during the 1970s, motivating Alaska Airlines to sell at a profit. In October 1980 Alaska Airlines sold Alyeska Resort to the Seibu Group, a Japanese conglomerate with the financial strength,

Anchorage Museum of History and Art

In 1961, skiers at Alyeska waited their turn to ride the chair lift.

experience, and commitment to develop a first-class, year-round resort. Chris von Imhof, who had been managing a Hawaii property for Seibu, returned to Alaska in 1995 to manage Alyeska. Seibu's expansion of the Alyeska resort has included the 307-room, chateau-style Alyeska Prince Hotel, which opened on August 26, 1994, and a gondola to serve skiers in winter and tourists in summer. The gondola also provides access to the Seven Glaciers Restaurant, a gourmet dining room with spectacular views of Turnagain Arm.

Alyeska has hosted major ski races, including the 1964 Olympic Trials, the 1969 Junior Nationals, the 1973 World Cup Giant Slalom, the 1987 World Masters Championship, the 1993 World Junior Olympic Competition, and the 1997 U.S. Alpine Masters Championship. Downhill skier Tommy Moe, who won Gold and Silver medals in the 1994 Winter Olympics, spent his early teens skiing on the Alyeska slopes.

Anchorage skiers were introduced to another form of skiing when Fort Richardson was chosen as the site for the U.S. Army Biathlon training center in 1958. The climate and terrain proved to be ideally suited for cross-country skiing and biathlon, a military sport that combines cross-country skiing with target shooting. Military biathletes, like Dick Mize, settled in Anchorage and introduced cross-country skiing as a competitive sport in the schools. On January 14, 1964, parents and friends of the school cross-country teams organized the Nordic Ski Club of Anchorage to assist in holding races and developing trails in local parks. An extensive trail system, maintained jointly by the Nordic Skiing Association and the Municipal Department of Parks and Recreation, has developed over the years to include 115 kilometers of trails, groomed for both diagonal and skating techniques, with 50 kilometers lighted. The Kincaid Park trails have been the site of Junior, Senior, Biathlon, and Masters World and National cross-county events. Anchorage cross-country skiers have been represented on every Olympic team from 1964 to 1998. ■

Mister Secretary

Anchorage residents did not have "live" television on December 11, 1968 to watch their townsman, Walter J. Hickel, be introduced by President Richard Nixon as the new Secretary of the Interior, but they hoped his appointment would boost Alaskan prosperity. After years of standing by while outsiders molded their state's future, a real Alaskan would finally be a national decision maker. Hickel already had the distinction of being the first Anchorage resident to hold a powerful statewide political position when he narrowly beat incumbent Governor William A. Egan in 1966. Hickel, a former Golden Gloves welterweight boxer from Kansas, delighted in telling how he arrived in Anchorage in 1940 as a twenty-year-old with thirty-seven cents in his pocket—he would have gone to Australia instead if he had been old enough to get his own passport.

Anchorage Museum of History and Art

Gov. Walter J Hickel shares a moment with Ann Stevens, the late wife of Senator Ted Stevens. Hickel had appointed Stevens to the U.S. Senate.

The expansive optimism he found in Anchorage suited him. "At no time was there ever a fleeting thought in my mind that I had made the wrong choice in picking a new home," Hickel later wrote in his book *Who Owns America?*

When the population of Anchorage started to grow after World War

II, Hickel joined developers like Emil Pfeil, Carl Martin, and "Muktuk" Marston in building rental units, upscale residential developments like Turnagain by the Sea, and neighborhood shopping centers. Realizing the Alaska Highway and air routes to Europe and Asia would bring tourists to Alaska, Hickel opened the Anchorage Traveler's Inn, Alaska's first modern motel, in 1953. Two years later, the Hickel Construction Company built a similar facility in downtown Fairbanks.

During the 1950s, Hickel joined the Republican Party and the fight for statehood. In 1954, as Republican National Committeeman, he led a group of Alaskans to Washington, D.C. to confront President Dwight D. Eisenhower on the subject of statehood. He was in the Senate gallery when the Alaska Statehood Bill passed on June 30, 1958.

Hickel was in Japan as head of a State Chamber of Commerce trade mission when the 1964 Good Friday earthquake devastated the Turnagain area. Although land on the west end of downtown Anchorage near the L Street slide where he was planning to build a large hotel was termed unstable, Hickel went ahead anyway and started excavating in August 1964. The Captain Cook Hotel, which opened on June 17, 1965, was proclaimed by one pioneer Alaskan to be "the finest roadhouse on the trail."

The following year, Hickel turned the Hickel Investment Company over to his brother Vernon and announced that he was running for governor of Alaska. Although he was considered a 9-to-1 underdog, Hickel won the primary over Mike Stepovich and Bruce Kendall with the help of 4,265 volunteer "Workers for Wally." His opposition in the general election was Democrat Bill Egan, who many voters thought had already served the two consecutive terms allowed by the state constitution. (Egan had chosen to run on the technicality that his first term had not been a full one, since he had turned the governorship over to Lieutenant Governor Hugh Wade for several months while recovering in Seattle from abdominal surgery.) Although neither Stepovich nor Kendall campaigned for him, Hickel won the hotly contested election by 1,080 votes.

The new governor, a strong supporter for Alaskan growth, arrived in Juneau with determination to do everything in his power to foster oil development. To deal with the oil companies, Hickel hired Tom Kelly, a personal friend from Houston, who moved to Anchorage. Kelly, who had experience in oil exploration and knew how oil companies acted and reacted, worked to plan more lucrative oil lease sales. Kelly was largely responsible for orchestrating the Prudhoe Bay competitive lease sale that brought Alaska almost a billion dollars in 1969.

Not all of Hickel's attempts to facilitate oil development worked as well as hiring Kelly. Soon after the discovery of oil at Prudhoe Bay, Governor Hickel proposed to slash a highway to the North Slope. In an attempt to turn a winter trail into an all-season road, construction crews bulldozed into the permafrost. When the summer sun melted the surface, the road turned into a canal, which was derisively known as the "Hickel Highway."

Damage done by the "Hickel Highway," constructed without permits or public hearings, enraged environmentalists, who promptly registered their reservations when President Richard Nixon selected Hickel to be Secretary of the Interior. Hickel had supported Nixon at several Republican Conventions and served as one of ten "surrogate candidates" during Nixon's successful campaign.

On the day Nixon planned to introduce his cabinet selections, Hickel faced an agonizing decision. The death of Senator E.L. (Bob) Bartlett gave him the opportunity to choose between three important political positions. He could continue as governor of Alaska; he could resign and become Secretary of the Interior; or he could resign and allow his successor, Lieutenant Governor Keith Miller, to appoint him to succeed Bartlett as Alaska's senior senator. (Hickel had succeeded in getting the State Legislature to pass a bill allowing the governor to appoint a successor from either political party rather than being limited to the same party as the deceased senator.) Hickel, challenged by the opportunity to serve in the Nixon cabinet, appointed Anchorage attorney Ted Stevens as Bartlett's successor. Hickel resigned the governorship to become Secretary of the Interior.

Before he could take over the Interior Department, Hickel had to face Senate confirmation hearings. He started off on the wrong foot by telling the national media shortly before the confirmation hearings that he could undo Udall's land freeze by executive order. Hickel realized that he needed Native support to counteract the environmentalists' opposition, so he agreed to continue the freeze and use his influence to persuade Nixon to settle the land claims by giving the Alaska Natives 40 million acres and half a billion dollars.

With the help of his Alaskan allies, Hickel was confirmed, but his tenure as Secretary of the Interior was a stormy one. President Nixon, rather than the conservationists, turned out to be Hickel's adversary. When he went to Washington in 1969, student unrest over war in Vietnam was at its height. As the father of five sons, Hickel understood the concerns and criticized Vice President Agnew's tirades against unruly "effete snobs" on American campuses. He hoped the Nixon administration was sincerely committed to ending the Vietnam conflict when, on April 30, 1970, he attended a White House briefing and learned that Nixon was going to announce the invasion of Cambodia.

Student reactions to the widening of the Vietnam War culminated in the tragic shooting on the Kent State University campus on May 4. In an attempt to persuade President Nixon to show greater concern for the student protest, Hickel wrote him a letter protesting the administration's alienation of young people. The letter came to the attention of the national media and angered Nixon. It was soon evident that Hickel's days in the administration were limited. Nothing happened until after the November 1970 elections, during which Hickel campaigned actively for Republican candidates. Shortly after Thanksgiving, Nixon gave Hickel his termination notice; Hickel replied, "If I leave, it will be with an arrow in my heart, not a bullet in my back."

Hickel returned to Alaska in December 1970 in time to see Bill Egan, who defeated Keith Miller the previous November, inaugurated for another term as Alaska's governor. Hickel entered the Republican gubernatorial primary in both 1974 and 1978, only to be defeated by Naknek legislator and bush pilot Jay Hammond, who won two terms as governor.

While Hickel's political career was in abeyance during the 1970s, the hotel business flourished. The discovery of North Slope oil and activity associated with pipeline construction boosted commercial travel and tourism. A second tower of the Captain Cook Hotel opened in 1974, providing 222 additional rooms and suites, the Discovery Ballroom, the Pantry Coffee Shop, and three meeting rooms in the lower lobby. A third phase of construction, Tower III, opened in 1978, bringing the capacity of the hotel to 600 rooms. Hickel family members managed the hotel with its fourteen meeting rooms, award-winning restaurant overlooking the city from the twentieth floor, and Athletic Club.

Hickel spent the next decade promoting building a natural gas pipeline from the North Slope to Valdez and continued to be active in Anchorage business affairs. He joined Bill Egan, who moved to Anchorage after losing the governorship to Hammond, in organizing Commonwealth North, a consortium of local business leaders who met regularly to hear visiting speakers and discuss pertinent issues of the day. After losing to State Senator Arliss Sturgelewski in the 1986 Republican primary, Hickel reappeared unexpectedly on the political scene in the 1990 election as candidate for governor on the Alaska Independence Party ticket. State Senator Arliss Sturgelewski had already won the nomination for governor in the Republican primary, and voters had selected State Senator Jack Coghill as her running mate. Coghill apparently did not want to run as second fiddle to a woman, so he persuaded Hickel to run for governor on the AIP ticket with him as candidate for lieutenant governor. The AIP candidate, John Lindauer, and his running mate stepped aside to make way for Hickel and Coghill. Hickel, who retained his popularity with Alaska conservatives, ran an energetic campaign and defeated both Sturgelewski and the Democratic candidate, Anchorage Mayor Tony Knowles.

In his 1991 State of the State address, Hickel announced his intention to combat the federal government. "It's time to let the word go out that no one dictates to us, and that we will not yield to outsiders what generations of Alaskans fought to create. It's time for Alaskans to take our country back." He instructed Attorney General Charles Cole to sue the federal government over conflicts between the Alaska National Lands Conservation Act and the Alaska Statehood Act and explained, "Our Statehood lawsuits are setting a precedent for the world. If the U.S. doesn't honor its contract with Alaska, it's a threat to our treaties with all other nations."

Governor Hickel attacked issues with the same spontaneous activism that he displayed during his first term as governor. In an attempt to push ahead on a road from Cordova to Chitina, he sent government highway maintenance crews in to upgrade the old Copper River and Northwestern Railroad right of way without bothering with environmental impact hearings. His philosophy, "There's no way a public hearing can design a road," didn't satisfy environmentalists, who promptly stopped the bulldozers with an injunction, claiming that they were polluting the Copper River. Hickel took credit for negotiating a legal settlement with Exxon Corporation for a billion-dollar to pay for impacts from the 1989 *Exxon Valdez* oil spill, but he did not push his idea to "lay a large diameter pipe on the ocean floor to carry fresh water from Alaska to drought-stricken California."

Hickel left the governorship in 1994 with some misgivings about Alaskans' complacency. His associate, Malcolm Roberts, included in *The Wit and Wisdom of Wally Hickel*, "There is no vision, no hope, no future, no agenda for Alaska, if your only ideology, if your only philosophy, if your only cause is to cut the budget.

"We used to say 'North to the future' in this state—and believed every word of it. We were always trying to prove our potential. We thought big ideas, and were willing to put in the grunt work to make these things happen. Today, I sense a different mood. Since Prudhoe Bay, which was the most exciting opportunity this state ever had to say 'yes' to the future, we have turned into a state of money changers.

"We've been so busy counting our money, we've lost our guts." ∎

9

The Oil Boom Years

Pipe for the 800-mile Trans-Alaska pipeline was purchased from Japan.

In order to capitalize on the 1969 Prudhoe Bay oil lease sale, oil companies needed to construct a pipeline to bring North Slope oil to market. Two obstacles stood in the way—Native land claims and concerns of conservationists. Passage of the Alaska Native Claims Settlement Act in 1971 resolved the land claims issue, and a 1973 Arab oil embargo counteracted conservationists' opposition. As soon as the construction permit for a pipeline from the North Slope to Valdez was issued, workers swarmed into Alaska. Anchorage's economy, although not directly on the pipeline route, boomed. Oil executives moved to town, and pipeline workers spent money in Anchorage during their time off.

In anticipation of future oil revenues, Alaskans voted to move the state capital from Juneau to a new community along the Railbelt and established a permanent fund in which to invest part of the new money. Oil revenues started coming into the state treasury after completion of the pipeline in 1977.

While Alaskans deliberated on the location of a new capital city, Anchorage residents approved a new municipal charter, eliminating duplication of services by the city and the Greater Anchorage Area Borough, and made plans to utilize some of the new state money to improve local facilities. Rapid population growth in Anchorage continued with an estimated 180,000 people residing in the Municipality of Anchorage area when the city and borough were unified in 1975.

Two weeks after Congressional committees approved lifting the land freeze to allow building of an oil pipeline, President Nixon signed the National Environmental Policy Act, which required an environmental impact statement for any project on federal land. In March 1970, five Native villages located north of the Yukon River filed a suit claiming ownership of land intended for the pipeline under their aboriginal claims. The following month environmental groups filed another federal suit to block pipeline construction, contending that the pipeline violated the National Environmental Policy Act.

These lawsuits persuaded the oil companies to help solve the Native land claims issue and get Natives as allies when they addressed environmental issues. With lobbying assistance from oil companies, Native groups succeeded in convincing Congress to pass the Alaska Native Claims Settlement Act (ANCSA). The settlement, which President Nixon signed into law on December 18, 1971, gave Alaskan Natives 44 million acres of land and $962.5 million. Congress adopted a plan proposed by the Alaska Federation of Natives, which established Native-owned corporations to give Alaska Natives an opportunity for self-determination. ANSCA provided that all persons with a minimum of one-quarter Native blood residing in Alaska enroll in

Anchorage Daily Times/Anchorage Daily News

Exxon sent the SS Manhattan through the Arctic Ocean to test using tankers to transport North Slope oil. The test proved the necessity of building the Trans-Alaska pipeline.

one of twelve regional corporations, as well as the village corporation in their community of residence. When the rolls were closed, approximately 76,000 persons claiming Alaska Native ancestry were given shares in their regional and village corporations.

Alaskan Natives living in Anchorage, the Matanuska-Susitna area, and parts of the Kenai Peninsula were included in Cook Inlet Region Incorporated (CIRI) and Eklutna Natives formed Eklutna, Inc. In addition to the money these two corporations funneled into the Anchorage economy, other regional and village corporations invested in Anchorage projects. The Bristol Bay Native Corporation, based in Dillingham, purchased the Anchorage-Westward Hotel and arranged for Hilton Hotels to manage the facility. Calista Corporation, consisting of forty villages centered in the Yukon-Kuskokwim Delta, constructed the hotel that became the Anchorage Sheraton and developed Settler's Bay subdivision across Knik Arm. Although these projects were not financially successful for Calista, the hotel construction contributed to the Anchorage economy and local residents profited from the first-class Sheraton Hotel and a scenic golf course at Settler's Bay. In addition to CIRI, which erected a large building in midtown to house its corporate headquarters, both Chugach Alaska Corporation and the Aleutian-Pribilof Corporation built headquarters buildings in Anchorage.

Even with the land issue settled, environmental challenges delayed pipeline construction until mid-1973, when an energy crisis prompted Congress to act. Controversy continued about whether the pipeline should be located entirely in Alaska, passing from the North Slope to Valdez, or should traverse Canada to supply oil to the United States Midwest, where it was most needed. Oil companies favored the trans-Alaska route, discounting arguments of an oil surplus on the West Coast and that tanker travel from Valdez was environmentally hazardous. To appease Midwestern congressmen, the Senate approved the trans-Alaska pipeline route with an amendment banning export of Alaskan oil to foreign countries. The Senate then narrowly approved Alaska Senator Mike Gravel's amendment to waive provisions of the National Environment Policy Act and prohibit further court challenges to the pipeline. The pipeline authorization bill was signed into law on November 16, 1973, by President Nixon.

Six years after the announcement of the Prudhoe Bay oil discovery, the Alyeska Pipeline Consortium was finally ready to start construction on the 369-mile Haul Road from the Yukon River to Prudhoe Bay. On March 27, 1975, the first pipe was installed. A mass of job seekers descended on Alaska after reading articles that quoted $1,200 weekly wages for pipeline workers. Alyeska's office in Anchorage received 6,576 letters and 1,370 phone calls in one month. Since some pipeline jobs required skilled workers, many came from the Texas and Oklahoma oil fields. Southern drawls and cowboy boots replaced mukluks on the streets of Anchorage, and Southern Baptist churches flourished. Pipeline work presented opportunities for Alaskans as well. Students and Natives joined experienced construction workers in the pipeline camps; women constituted about ten percent of the work force. Inflated pipeline salaries enticed workers to leave service jobs in town. High school students found it easy to find after-school jobs.

Pipeline workers left camp every nine weeks for rest and relaxation with thousands of dollars in their pockets. Some passed through Anchorage to take flights back home or to vacation in Hawaii, while others spent their time and money in town. Gambling and prostitution became significant problems. When Fairbanks passed an ordinance banning "loitering for the purposes of prostitution," some of its "girls of the night" joined those already operating in Anchorage. A commission appointed by Mayor George Sullivan to study prostitution estimated 215 prostitutes were working in the city, mostly in massage parlors.

Although counteracting the vices that accompanied the pipeline boom and dealing with increased road traffic strained public services, Anchorage benefited from investments made by pipeline workers and oil executives. Some bought real estate and built houses or started small businesses. Fairbanks attempted to entice oil companies to leave Anchorage and establish headquarters closer to the North Slope, but the more favorable climate and other amenities made them reluctant to leave. Oil executives and their families contributed to the quality of life in town with monetary support and volunteer work.

Once the pipeline was under construction, speed was essential; oil companies realized they lost revenue during the construction period. Construction contracts were negotiated on a cost-plus basis because economy was not a consideration. Pipeline workers demanded good food. Lavish spreads in the dining halls included steak, frog legs, beef Wellington, lobster, and prime rib. Careful controls were not kept on tools, equipment, and supplies. Pipeline workers are reported to have built cabins and furnished houses and businesses with discarded supplies.

The pipeline was completed in three years and two months at a cost of $8 billion. A total of 70,000 workers were employed on pipeline construction from 1969 to 1977, with peak employment of 28,072 in October 1975. Alyeska Pipeline Consortium had succeeded and Anchorage had changed.

Joe McGinness described Anchorage of the mid-seventies in his book, *Going To Extremes*: "Anchorage was a boom town, nervous and greedy, afraid that the music would stop, afraid that the money would run out. A town of Texans and Teamsters and pickup trucks, bars and liquor stores, pawnshops and guns, country music, massage parlors, Baptist churches, public drunkenness, and an alarming rate of automobile accidents. But there were new restaurants, too, with wine lists and fresh flowers on the table. And new office buildings rising fast. With the oil had come the professional classes— lawyers and stockbrokers and real estate developers....Anchorage was a city that had got a late start; now it was trying to catch up all at once, skipping about two hundred years. It was poised on the edge, between its past, which was not much, and a future which was expected to be everything. Poised also between the "real Alaska," or, at least, rural Alaska, and the cosmopolitan capitals of the world.

John McPhee, who also visited Alaska in the mid-seventies and wrote *Coming Into the Country*, was less complementary when he described Anchorage as "condensed, instant Albuquerque" and as "an American spore." McPhee wrote about the national interest lands in Alaska that were being considered for withdrawal under the d-2 provision of the Alaska Native Claims Settlement Act and about the 1974 proposal to move the capital from Juneau to a new city between Anchorage and Fairbanks.

As the population of Anchorage grew following World War II, people in Southcentral Alaska became increasingly irritated that the center of state government remained in a city that could only be reached by air or sea. Throughout the sixties, Editor Robert Atwood of the *Anchorage Daily Times* advocated moving the capital to Anchorage. In both 1960 and 1962, capital move initiatives had been defeated. The danger of flying into the Juneau airport, which is surrounded by high mountains and often shrouded in rain and fog, became real in September 1971, when an Alaska Airlines Boeing 727 crashed on approach to Juneau, killing 7 crew members and 104 passengers. The possibility a large number of government officials and legislators could be wiped out in an airline crash again stimulated talk about moving the capital to a more accessible location. When Anchorage State Senator Frank Harris introduced the 1974 capital move initiative, he hoped to capture the Fairbanks vote by stipulating that the

Workers completed ironwork for the tower of the Anchorage Westward Hotel in March 1971.

capital be located in the Railbelt area between the two cities but at least thirty miles away from either one. With anticipation that oil money would be adequate to build a "Brasilia in the north," fifty-seven percent of state voters approved the initiative and the governor appointed a nine-member Capital Site Selection Committee to study potential sites from which the voters would select the new capital. McPhee accompanied the com-

161

mittee members as they visited the three sites to be presented to the electorate—Willow, 80 miles northwest of Anchorage; Larson Lake, 120 miles north of Anchorage near Talkeetna; and Mt. Yenlo, farther west near Skwentna. After voters chose the Willow site in 1976, land speculators subdivided unoccupied tracts in the Matanuska and Susitna Valleys, architectural firms submitted plans for the new capital city, and the state studied the feasibility of damming the Susitna River to provide hydroelectric power. In April 1977, capital move opponents launched a petition drive to get an initiative on the 1978 ballot requiring Alaskans to approve a bond issue for relocation of the capital before it could be moved.

All Alaskans were not as committed to rapid development as the *Anchorage Times*, the Teamster's Union, and a majority of Anchorage businessmen. Former State Senator Jay Hammond from Naknek, a Bristol Bay fishing community, won the 1974 Republican primary supporting "healthy vs. malignant growth." Hammond defeated two former governors, Wally Hickel and Keith Miller, in the primary, and then won the general election by a narrow margin over former Governor William A. Egan. Hammond ran for reelection in 1978, and he defeated Hickel in the primary and Democratic State Senator Chancey Croft of Anchorage in the general election. In this general election, Hickel, unwilling to accept his narrow defeat in the primary, ran an unsuccessful statewide write-in campaign. Although opponents labeled the new governor "Zero Growth Hammond," Alaska's economy thrived during his two terms. The most notable achievement of Hammond's first term was the creation of the Alaska Permanent Fund in which the state would deposit at least a quarter of nonrenewable resource earnings with provisions for increases dependent on future earnings.

While the state government was joyfully contending with the problems of becoming a wealthy state, Anchorage was solving its own government problems. The Alaska Constitutional Convention had established the borough form of government to prevent duplication of services. In Anchorage, however, the City of Anchorage and the Greater Anchorage Area Borough continually bickered over governmental responsibilities. When the second-class borough was established in 1964, it automatically assumed area-wide powers of planning and zoning, education, property assessment, and tax collection. By 1975, voters had added an area-wide sewer system, building code enforcement, fire prevention and suppression, transit, and parks and recreation to the borough's responsibilities. The city saw the borough as trying to eliminate the city completely, and the borough accused the city of trying to expand directly into the borough by annexation. The borough assembly had eleven members, with six members elected from the non-city area and five members appointed from the city council. Several of the non-city members represented "rural" areas that opposed the borough's acquiring new powers, and the city members often voted as a bloc to restrict borough functions.

The possibility of unifying the borough and the city was discussed as early as 1966. A City-Borough Study Committee concluded in 1969: "1) There are duplications of effort and confused authority which can only increase as the area grows; 2) Better or more services can be offered on an area wide basis and on a service area basis by a single form of government; 3) The capital improvement needs of the area can best be met by a single agency responsible for coordination of planning and financing; and 4) The economy of the entire area as well as political, social, and cultural life is an entity which transcends subordinate boundary lines."

The cause for unification gained momentum with help from the Operation Breakthrough Committee and the League of Women Voters. In October 1969, voters approved the concept of unification and elected an eleven-member charter commission, which prepared a charter with the help of Public Administration Service, the nonprofit firm that had assisted the framers of the state constitution. The charter, which was presented to voters in August 1970, was approved in the city but turned down outside the city. A second attempt to pass a unification charter in 1971 also failed. The issue remained dormant until November 7, 1974, when the borough assembly voted to put unification and charter commission propositions on the February 1975 election ballot.

When the unification concept was approved in 1975, Chugiak-Eagle River area residents did not vote because they were attempting to form a borough of their own. The Chugiak-Eagle River area reluctantly joined the new Municipality of Anchorage on April 15, 1976, when the Alaska

Supreme Court declared legislation creating the Chugiak-Eagle River Borough unconstitutional because the area was not large enough to warrant a new borough. When the unification charter was approved by 66.9% of voters area-wide on September 11, 1976, only 27.8% of the Chugiak-Eagle River voters approved.

The first action of the new Municipality of Anchorage was the election of a mayor, and city Mayor George Sullivan defeated borough Mayor Jack Roderick. Sullivan stressed competence and picked his staff from both former city and borough officials. The new management team faced an overwhelming task of creating a completely new governmental structure out of two existing ones. There were two personnel systems with seventeen major and forty minor differences in salary structures, classification plans, and benefits. There were nine different union contracts and different fiscal years and budgets.

Municipal responsibilities increased during the late seventies to provide services for the ballooning population. Parks and recreation services received a special boost in 1976, when the federal government gave the municipality a 5,000-acre tract that had been used as an auxiliary airfield during World War II. This tract, known as Far North Bicentennial Park, provided residents with a wilderness park in the center of the municipality where they can enjoy hiking, cross-country skiing, horseback riding, mountain biking, and nature study. The Hilltop Ski Area, developed in the southeast corner of Bicentennial Park, provided easily accessible novice ski slopes serviced by a chair lift. Bicentennial Park connected to the 495,000-acre Chugach State Park, which was established by the state legislature in the early 1970s. Trailheads with parking lots provided Anchorage residents access to a vast mountain wilderness. In 1979 the Municipal Parks and Recreation Department took over management of 1,500-acre Kincaid Park when the federal government turned over the former military site at Point Campbell.

Writer John McPhee noted that Anchorage "might be a sorry town, but it has the greatest out-of-town any town ever had." After unification this great "out-of-town" became part of the Municipality of Anchorage. ■

Jesse Carr: Boss of the Teamsters

Teamsters Local 959, led by Jesse L. Carr, reached its greatest influence during pipeline construction in the 1970s. News reports in 1975 estimated the union had 23,000 members, including Anchorage policemen and hospital workers as well as pipeline truck drivers, roughnecks, drillers, and longshoremen. At the heights of its membership, the Teamsters banked about $1 million a week in its pension trust accounts. Secretary-Treasurer Carr knew how to apply muscle to pipeline contractors, coercing them into hiring hundreds of extra workers in the name of safety and labor peace. He once demanded that Teamster-driven pilot cars accompany all trucks on the haul road and that two Teamsters sit in each base ambulance twenty-four hours a day. Alyeska Pipeline Consortium was so anxious to complete the pipeline rapidly that it did nothing to provoke the Teamsters.

A high school dropout who served in the Marines during World War II, Carr arrived in Alaska in 1950. He had joined the Teamsters in California as a truck driver and soon became business agent for Local 959. As a result of a close association with West Coast Teamster boss Dave Beck in the late 1950s, Carr was granted autonomy in Alaska with relative independence from the international union. The union's growth continued steadily for the next decade during Swanson River and Cook Inlet oil exploration. Although Carr was charged in the late 1960s with extortion, embezzlement, and making false statements in obtaining a government loan, he was cleared on all counts, without any of them reaching a jury. Four counts were dismissed on a directed verdict of acquittal by U.S. District Court Judge James A. von der Heydt. Prosecutors dropped the remaining two counts because the government's key witness was too ill to testify.

Investigation of Teamster activities by the *Anchorage Daily News* won a 1975 Pulitzer Prize. Rumors of Teamster ties to organized crime spread the following summer when two Teamster shop stewards were abducted from the Fairbanks pipeline warehouse. Their bullet-ridden bodies were found weeks later. The state's inability to crack down on pipeline crime brought the FBI to Alaska in a cleanup effort. After two years of investigation, nine persons were indicted, but all were acquitted.

With $1 million a week flowing into Local 959's trust accounts, the largest being the pension fund, Carr saw an opportunity to build an empire, but he trampled on key provisions of the Employee Retirement Income Security Act of 1974 (ERISA). He organized a nonprofit subsidiary called Teamsters Local 959 Building Corporation and went on a construction spree. The Teamsters erected the 200-bed Alaska Hospital in Anchorage at a cost of $32 million where Union members, presumably, would receive free care. Local 959 hired administrators to employ doctors willing to negotiate fees. Adjoining the hospital, Local 959 built a 4,000-square-foot professional building and the Teamsters Mall to house shops, restaurants, and bank branches. At another Anchorage site on Tudor Road, the Teamsters erected a modern recreation center with an indoor pool, tennis courts, an indoor running track, and a well-equipped body building room. Alongside the recreation center, the seven-story Jesse L. Carr office complex housed Teamster headquarters. Similar facilities in Fairbanks were planned, but only the recreation center had been built before pipeline construction ended and Teamster influence waned.

Elizabeth Tower

This office building, named after Teamster leader Jesse Carr, was one of several union investments that went sour as the Alaska and Anchorage economies plunged after completion of the Trans-Alaska Pipeline.

The Local 959 empire was not limited to Alaska. Tapping the pension fund, Carr built the $120-million Desert Horizons country club-condominium development in Indian Wells, California, near Palm Springs. He asked the union members to consider the country club a shrewd investment and purchased a Lear Jet for regular trips to oversee the property. While they lived modestly in Anchorage, Carr and his wife bought a large condominium near Desert Horizons and hosted union power brokers.

Carr's fortunes started to change in the early 1980s. With the pipeline built, Teamsters began leaving Alaska, drastically reducing revenues. By the end of 1979, the Teamster building corporation had a deficit of $6.8 million. The Alaska Hospital lost money at an alarming rate. Growing dissatisfaction within Teamster ranks surfaced in 1981 during a strike against Anchorage Cold Storage, the state's largest wholesale distributor of meats, beverages, and grocery products. Carr's attempts to coerce all Teamster union members to support the strike with picketing assessments was ruled illegal, and Cold Storage employees decertified the union. In the meantime, the Department of Labor charged violations of ERISA in most of the Teamster pension fund investments in Alaska. The union was ordered to begin disposing of investments immediately. The Humana Hospital chain bought the hospital within the year. Recreation centers in both Anchorage and Fairbanks were sold to a group of private investors and continue to function.

By 1983, the Teamsters were still $4.2 million in debt and membership dropped to 12,000. Carr's drive for power in the international union continued, but his frequent trips to California came to an unexpected quick end. On January 5, 1985, the fifty-nine-year-old union boss was found dead on the living room floor of his Indian Wells home. A coroner's inquiry attributed his death to heart failure.

The collapse of the Anchorage real estate market in 1986 proved Local 959's final undoing. It filed for Chapter 11 bankruptcy before the year was out. The decline of the Alaska Teamsters Union paralleled the decline of the union in the rest of the country. The Alaska union is now a mere shadow of its former self, with a 70 percent drop in membership from its peak. ∎

Anchorage's Strong Mayor

George M. Sullivan was the Municipality of Anchorage's first "strong mayor," as defined by the 1975 unification charter. Earlier noteworthy mayors—Z.J. Loussac, Elmer Rasmuson, and George Sharrock—served along with city managers, who were responsible for much of the city's day-to-day operation. Sullivan bore the burden of creating an entirely new government out of two existing ones—the City of Anchorage and the Greater Anchorage Area Borough.

Sullivan, like William A. Egan, Alaska's first governor, and Delegate to Congress Anthony J. Dimond, came from Valdez. Although both Egan and Dimond ended their careers in Anchorage and have local buildings named for them, they are still thought of as Valdez residents. Sullivan's name, on the other hand, will always be associated with Anchorage because of the pivotal role he played in the development of the modern municipality.

Anchorage Museum of History and Art

As mayor of Anchorage, George Sullivan commemorated the city's 50th anniversary of self rule in 1970.

Sullivan attributes his interest in politics and his political savvy to his parents and to his boyhood in Valdez. His father, Harvey, and four uncles crossed the Chilkoot Pass during the 1898 gold rush. After scratching around Dawson for several years, the elder Sullivan moved on to Nome, where he mined on the beaches. In 1907 Harvey Sullivan, a lifelong Republican, was appointed United States Marshal and moved to Valdez, where he married George's mother, Viola.

The Third Division Federal Court was based in Valdez while George Sullivan and Bill Egan were growing up, and attendance at court sessions was included in the school curriculum. Republican George and Democrat Bill frequently engaged in political debates, with George occasionally receiving coaching from his mother in order to counteract the arguments of Egan, who was seven years older. Viola Sullivan served a term as the mayor of Valdez, the first woman mayor of an Alaskan city.

George hoped to become a lawyer, but both his parents died while he was still in his teens and he had to work at various jobs to help support his family: longshoring, mining, and road construction in Valdez; unloading ore buckets at the Kennecott Copper Mine; and construction during the building of Fort Richardson. During World War II, he served in the Aleutian Islands, rising rapidly in the ranks and receiving army commendation.

Following the war, Sullivan settled in Fairbanks, where he married Margaret Eagan in 1946. An appointment as United States Marshal took the young couple to Nenana for five years, during which George monitored a strike at the Healy coal mines. They subsequently moved back to Fairbanks, where Sullivan managed a DEW-Line contract on the Arctic Coast for Alaska Freight Lines during the winter of 1954-55.

Sullivan's introduction to local politics occurred in 1955, when he was appointed to fill out a term on the Fairbanks City Council. He resigned in 1959 to move to Anchorage as manager of Consolidated Freightways. When Sullivan left Fairbanks, the Fairbanks City Council took out a full-page ad in the *Anchorage Times* saying that their loss was Anchorage's gain. Sullivan was introduced to state politics in 1963, when Governor Egan appointed him to complete a term in the state legislature, representing Anchorage-at-large. Since Sullivan missed daily contact with his constituents while he was serving in Juneau, he opted to enter local politics again and was elected to the Anchorage City Council in 1965. He was elected mayor in 1967.

During Sullivan's two terms as mayor of the City of Anchorage, rivalry between the city and the Greater Anchorage Area Borough intensified. Attempts to adopt a unification charter failed in 1970 and 1972, but succeeded in 1975. The new charter permitted Sullivan to run again, and he defeated borough Mayor Jack Roderick to become the first mayor of the Municipality of Anchorage. With the pipeline boom at its height and an expanding Anchorage population placing increased demands on local government, Mayor Sullivan faced the additional task of creating a new administration. In a July 1981 interview for *Alaska Industry*, he described his first days in office. "There were just a million things to do, and it meant that there were no department heads in any positions. It meant that the ordinances had to be brought together and codified. It meant that at that time we had eleven unions that we finally brought down to six, but the differences in union contracts between the two governments were substantial. You had two separate sets of personnel rules, you had two separate legal departments, two separate finance departments. All of these I had to bring together in some type of cohesion."

Mayor Sullivan interviewed hundreds of people and built his administration with a combination of former city and borough employees plus some new ones. He faced Teamster boss Jesse Carr at the bargaining table and earned the reputation of being a tough union negotiator. As strong mayor of the municipality, Sullivan had veto power that he did not have when he was city mayor. He occasionally used that power and none of his vetoes were overridden by the assembly.

Mayor Sullivan realized the State of Alaska would be receiving billions of dollars of new revenue once the oil started flowing through the Trans-Alaska Pipeline. He wanted to make sure Anchorage would get its share of the oil money to use for something long-lasting that people would remember, so he and his staff developed a long list of capital improvements. They approached the state legislature and received a $157 million grant in 1980, followed by additional grants of $235 million. Completion of the Project 80's capital improvements was left to Sullivan's successor, since the municipal charter limits the mayor to two terms. The original Project 80's buildings include the William A. Egan Civic and Convention Center; the Alaska Center for the Performing Arts; the Town Square; major expansion of the Anchorage Museum of History and Art; a new Loussac Library; the George M. Sullivan Sports Arena; a large city transit facility; a new animal control shelter; the Dempsey Anderson ice arena; the Spenard Recreation Center; the Fire Lake ice arena in Eagle River; and expansion of the Senior Center in Chugiak. Project 80's funds also provided an Olympic-sized swimming pool at Bartlett High School; the Anchorage Golf Course; an equestrian center; the Hilltop Ski Area; expansion of Kincaid Park and Hillside cross-country ski trails, ski jumps, and chalet; and the Tony Knowles Coastal Trail.

After George Sullivan passed the reins to Tony Knowles in 1982, he served as a vice president of Western Airlines and was involved in the management of Multi-Visions. ■

Anchorage Museum of History and Art

Mayor George Sullivan was known for addressing problems when he saw them, including picking up a bit of trash when he saw it.

Skyjacking, Alaskan Style

With planes leaving daily for European and Asian cities, Anchorage had prided itself on being the "air crossroads of the world," but an episode on October 18, 1971 riveted worldwide attention on Alaskan aviation. At 4:30 a.m. a young man approached the ticket agent at Alaska Airlines to buy a ticket. The agent was suspicious when the man seemed uncertain about his destination. She did not tell him an Alaska Airlines flight was about to leave for Seattle, but told him a Wien Consolidated Airline 737 would leave for Bethel, a Native village on the Kuskokwim River, at 5:30 a.m. Wien did not screen passengers with metal detectors; no one considered Alaska "bush" flights to be likely skyjacking targets.

The Monday morning plane to Bethel regularly carried villagers returning home and government officials traveling on business. Among the thirty-one passengers on the flight were an Alaska Native Medical Center orthopedic surgeon traveling to hold a clinic and an Alaska Federation of Natives planner. Shortly after the plane reached cruising altitude, the young man approached a flight attendant with a small automatic pistol and said, "This plane isn't going to Bethel!"

Nancy Davis, the twenty-two-year-old flight attendant, was making her first flight as a stewardess, and she was the daughter of Western Airlines Captain Charles Davis. Capt. Davis once successfully landed a plane after an engine fell off and had been involved in developing airline safety procedures. Nancy applied to Wien on the advice of her brother, a Wien pilot, because she wanted to see more of Alaska. After two weeks training, she received her wings the evening before the Bethel flight.

Since Nancy had just reviewed the new Wien hijack regulations, she gave the pilot the hijack code. The rest of the crew thought she was kidding at first, but was convinced of her seriousness when the hijacker threatened to shoot the plane's windows. Most passengers were unaware of the situation. At first the hijacker was unsure where he wanted to go; Nancy managed to persuade him that the plane could fly farther if it refueled in Anchorage and reduced the load by letting passengers off. Nancy felt she had established good rapport with the hijacker and insisted on staying, so the senior flight attendant deplaned with the passengers.

After refueling, the hijacker decided to go to Cuba. The plane had a range of about 2,000 miles, they had to refuel in Vancouver, B.C. and make another refueling stop in Mexico. Nancy persuaded the hijacker to show her the gun was loaded. She suspected that he was on drugs and continued to feed him coffee as they talked. When he requested stronger beverages, she convinced him, erroneously, that morning flights were not supplied with alcohol. He explained he had just been paroled from the minimal security center in Palmer after serving five years of a twenty-year sentence for manslaughter in Kodiak.

After the plane left Vancouver for Mexico at 11:43 a.m., the hijacker and stewardess continued talking about his future. She convinced him he would probably face prison wherever he went and conditions would be better for him in Canada, where he could speak the language. Two hours later, when the plane was over Salt Lake City, the hijacker agreed to return to Vancouver. After a long talk with a Canadian Mounted Police representative, the hijacker permitted the Wien crew to leave the plane. Later, he was returned to Anchorage, where he was convicted of air piracy and returned to prison.

The skyjacking episode was a turning point in Nancy Davis's career. She continued to fly for Wien for another year, during which she survived four forced landings and satisfied her desire to see "bush Alaska." In 1972 she married Cliff Hollenbeck, the Wien public relations officer at the time of the skyjacking. They got to know each other while arranging interviews with Walter Cronkite and other television anchormen. Shortly after the Wien episode, the crew members were flown to New York to participate along with other hijacked crews in a United Nations attempt to abolish safe havens for hijackers. Nancy convinced them to include her father in these deliberations because his experience had been such a profound influence on her. She received commendations both in Alaska and nationally.

After Cliff and Nancy married, they spent a year as photojournalists in Thailand covering the end of the Vietnam War. They returned to North America and spent a year developing an air safety manual for Canada before establishing their own photojournalism business in Seattle. ■

Iditarod: "A Spectacular Dog Race"

Alaskans have always had a love affair with sled dogs, and Anchorage is no exception. Early twentieth-century Nome residents discovered sled dogs could be used for sport as well as transportation. Leonhard Seppala and A.A. "Scotty" Allan became heroes of the Nome sweepstakes races. More recently George Attla and Roxy Wright Champaine, among others, were repeat winners of the Anchorage Fur Rendezvous sprint races. None of these champions, however, have captured the sporting world attention like the mushers who run the 1,049-mile Iditarod Race from Anchorage to Nome each March.

The Iditarod Race was initially promoted by Dorothy Page, a self-described history buff, who served as president of the Wasilla-Knik Centennial Committee in 1966. Her primary task was to organize an event to celebrate the 100th anniversary of the purchase of Alaska from Russia. She wanted to stage "a spectacular dog race to wake Alaskans up to what mushers and their dogs had done for Alaska," but she was having difficulty selling her idea until she met Joe Redington Sr. at the Willow Winter Carnival.

Redington and his family had driven to Alaska from Oklahoma in 1948. Shortly after crossing the border, a service station owner gave them a puppy—a harbinger of things to come. The Redingtons bought land in Knik which was adjacent to the historic Iditarod Trail used by prospectors to travel from Southcentral Alaska to gold fields at Iditarod and Nome at the start of the century. By the end of his first year in Alaska, Redington owned forty dogs and had started Knik Kennels. At first he used the dogs for work rather than sport. They hauled logs for cabins and participated in rescue missions for the military. When he had time, Redington brushed out portions of the old trail and lobbied successfully to have it added to the National Historic Trails System. Redington responded enthusiastically to Page's idea of a centennial race and insisted that the event should offer $25,000 in prize money, which was considerably more than the $6,700 purse for the Anchorage Fur Rendezvous race. The 1967 Iditarod race,

Anchorage crowds watch the start of the Iditarod Race in 1990. The annual race is recognized as the premier distance sled dog race in the world.

which was run in two twenty-five-mile heats, attracted an all-star field of fifty-eight mushers. The race was officially named the Iditarod Trail Seppala Memorial Race, in honor of mushing legend Leonhard Seppala, who had participated in the mercy serum run to Nome in 1925, even though the serum run, which was from Nenana to Nome, didn't actually use the old Iditarod trail. The winner, Isaac Okleasik from Teller, received $7,000 for his efforts.

The race was canceled in 1968 due to lack of snow. When it was reinstated in 1969 with $1,000 prize money, only twelve mushers participated and interest in the race waned. Redington persisted with his "impossible dream" of a long-distance race to Nome. In 1973 the first race to Nome with $51,000 prize money was won by Dick Wilmarth from Red Devil on the Kuskokwim River in twenty days. The field consisted of thirty-four teams; twenty-two of them successfully reached Nome. Wilmarth's lead dog, Hot Foot, got loose in Nome but managed to return 500 miles to Red Devil on his own.

In spite of periodic opposition from animal lovers claiming cruelty to dogs, the Iditarod Race has flourished through the years and has earned international fame as "The Last Great Race on Earth." Journalists from throughout the United States and overseas have reported from the trail. Television networks have covered the race and produced post-race specials. The majority of entrants continue to be Alaskan, but mushers from the rest of the United States, Canada, Norway, Switzerland, New Zealand, Great Britain, Australia, Germany, Italy, Japan, France, Austria, and Russia have also participated. The majority of the mushers have been men, but women have been well represented by top contenders Susan Butcher, Libby Riddles, and Dee Dee Jonrowe. Joe Redington Sr. has been a regular competitor in the race, frequently finishing in the top ten even when he was in his seventies.

There have been some notable changes in the Iditarod Race through the years. Mushers are required to prove their ability by participating in one of a series of 300-mile warm-up races; rest periods are mandatory during the race. Veterinarians make sure that dogs are properly immunized, and examine them periodically during the race to determine their health. The actual start of the race was moved to Wasilla when the trail from Anchorage proved dangerous because of poor snow cover and increased road traffic. The ceremonial start in Anchorage, however, is a great media event on the first Saturday morning in March. Although weather and snow conditions influence the time required to reach Nome each year, mushers generally arrive on the Bering coast in half the time it took Wilmarth back in 1973. ■

10

A Decade of Prosperity

Elizabeth Tower

Anchorage retains a large amount of natural open space within the city. Joggers, bikers, and runners enjoy the city skyline from the fourteen mile Tony Knowles Coastal Trail.

In the early 1980s local governments and individuals began to benefit from the influx of oil money. At the instigation of Mayor George Sullivan, Anchorage had already developed a list of desired capital improvement projects and local legislators acquired state grants to start construction on Project 80's. Individuals began receiving oil revenue directly in 1982 when the state legislature instituted the Alaska Permanent Fund dividend program. Both state and local government executives changed in 1982 with William Sheffield, an Anchorage hotel owner, replacing Governor Hammond, and Mayor Sullivan turning the municipal administration over to Tony Knowles. By 1981, Anchorage was growing by 1,000 people a month and experiencing a housing boom, which continued until 1986 when the price of crude oil collapsed. Between 1987 and 1989, Alaska lost 20,000 jobs and real estate values fell by up to fifty percent. The *Exxon Valdez* environmental disaster was a savior for the state's economic recovery.

Alaskan oil development proponents suffered a setback in 1980 when Congress passed the Alaska National Interest Lands Conservation Act (ANILCA), which set aside 104 million acres as national park land and wildlife refuges. Included in the lands set aside was the Alaska National Wildlife Refuge (ANWR), adjacent to the Prudhoe Bay oil fields, where oil companies expected to discover additional oil reserves. Capital move advocates were also thwarted. A statewide vote in 1982 failed to authorize bonds necessary to start construction on a new capital city near Willow. For the time being, at least, the state capital would remain in Juneau. Nothing, on the other hand, blocked an Anchorage building boom that rivaled the military construction of the 1940s.

The George M. Sullivan Sports Area, with a seating capacity of 5,788, was the first of the Project 80's buildings to be completed. This large facility provided space that could be adapted for hockey games, circuses, and rodeos as well as trade shows. On Thanksgiving weekend in 1983, the University of Alaska Anchorage moved the popular yearly Great Alaska Shootout to the Sullivan Arena. The Shootout brings top college basketball teams from around the United States to compete in a three-day elimination tournament with the local UAA Seawolves.

The $27-million Egan Civic and Convention Center opened in February 1984, three months before the death of William A. Egan, Alaska's first elected governor. Design changes delayed construction on the Performing Arts Center when Tony Knowles started his first three-year term as mayor. Although the existing Sydney Laurence Auditorium was to have been incorporated in the new complex, plans were altered by the new administration. The old auditorium was torn down and three new theaters were included in a new building. The 800-seat Discovery Theater was the first to open with a performance of Bizet's opera *Carmen*, and the 350-seat Sydney Laurence Theater was available for plays and ensemble concerts when the 2,100-seat Evangeline Atwood Theater opened in 1988 with a traveling production of the Broadway musical *Cats*. The Atwood Theater is the regular home of the Anchorage Symphony and provides a suitable facility for the Anchorage Concert Association to bring a variety of national and international performances to town.

The new Loussac Library in midtown was finally completed in 1986, but the planned underground parking had to be eliminated due to shortage of funds. An extension to the Anchorage Museum of History and Art was also finished in 1986, complete with underground parking. Other Project 80's buildings completed by 1987 included the Spenard Recreation Center, a 1,200-space downtown parking garage, the downtown Transit Center, and the Animal Control Center.

Carolyn A Strand

Kincaid Park's ski trails offer obstacles not found in most cities. Anchorage residents have learned to enjoy watching moose, while at the same time giving it plenty of space.

Mayor Tony Knowles was committed to providing recreational amenities for Anchorage as well as buildings. The appropriately named fourteen-mile Tony Knowles Coastal Trail lets joggers, dog-walkers, skiers, in-line skaters, and cyclists enjoy Cook Inlet views while going from downtown to Kincaid Park, where an extensive trail system and indoor sports center were opened in 1986. In the Chugach foothills southeast of town, the Hillside cross-country trail system and the Hilltop alpine ski area were also developed. The Dempsey Anderson and Fire Lake Ice Arenas were included in Project 80's to provide indoor ice for hockey and figure skaters. Both golfers and horseback riders got a piece of the action when the Anchorage Golf Course and the Equestrian Center opened in 1987 on Section 16 in the mid-Hillside area. Anchorage's first Olympic-size pool, erected at Bartlett High School, made it possible for swimmers to compete on the national level.

Private sector construction boomed in the early 1980s, with oil companies leading the way. ARCO's twenty-one-story downtown office building became the tallest building in town. The Hunt (Ensearch) Building in the downtown area and the BP and Frontier Buildings in midtown added new high-rise landmarks to the Anchorage skyline. Although three Anchorage major hotels planned to spend about $100 million and add over 1,000 beds, only the 200-room Anchorage Westward Hilton tower was actually built by 1986. Between 1980 and 1985, Anchorage added 25,000 new housing units, an increase of forty percent. Shopping malls appeared on almost every appropriately zoned corner and new subdivisions spread over the Anchorage bowl. In the mid-1980s Anchorage population exceeded 200,000.

The future looked very bright in 1985. Anchorage was honored as an All-American City for the third time in 1984. The following year, the United States Olympic Committee designated Anchorage as the United States choice to bid for the 1994 Winter Olympic Games. The Alaska Power Authority was planning for a $5.1 billion Susitna Dam Project to provide hydroelectric power for Southcentral Alaska. A final triumph in 1985 was the state purchase of the Alaska Railroad from the federal government for $22.3 million.

The railroad had several profitable seasons prior to state purchase,

Elizabeth Tower

The ARCO Building is reflected in the Ensearch Building downtown Anchorage. Most large office buildings were built during the oil boom of the 1980s.

although the passenger service still lost money. At the time of purchase, the railroad had title to 41,000 acres of Railbelt land and 650 miles of track in service, with 62 locomotives, 1,642 freight cars, and 46 passenger cars. The state delegated management to a seven-member quasi-public board of directors and indicated intent to spend $40 to $45 million on improvements to the railroad. Anchorage had become the undisputed

181

transportation hub of Alaska with the rapidly expanding Port of Anchorage and a developing air freight industry in addition to the railroad.

Purchase of the railroad was only one of many ways that the state found to spend its new-found wealth. When William Sheffield, owner of several Alaska hotels including the Travelodge and Sheffield House in Anchorage, replaced Governor Hammond in 1982, he was recognized as more development-oriented than his predecessor. The Alaska Permanent Fund was established during the Hammond administration before the oil bonanza began. When Permanent Fund investments started earning income the legislature decided to distribute these earnings to all Alaskans as dividends. The first dividend check of $1,000 was issued in 1982 to all adults and children who could prove residence in Alaska. The disposable income of Alaskans was further augmented because the legislature abolished the state income tax in 1980 when the state had adequate oil income to fund government programs. Anchorage residents were more fortunate than most other urban Alaskans because Anchorage never levied a sales tax.

Anchorage residents had the rare benefit during the 1980s of having two daily newspapers with divergent editorial policies. With the flourishing economy, many businesses advertised in both papers, and over a quarter of local households subscribed to both the morning *Anchorage Daily News* and the evening *Anchorage Daily Times*. The *Times*, the dominant paper in town since 1915, was conservative and pro-development. Editor Robert Atwood, often characterized as a "boomer," had been an early proponent of statehood and was the driving force behind efforts to move the capital to Southcentral Alaska. The *News*, started as a weekly by Norman Brown in 1946, received assistance from Cap Lathrop and his associates to start publishing the *Anchorage Daily News* on May 3, 1948. For the next decade the *News* attempted to neutralize the intensely pro-statehood editorial policy of the *Times*. After statehood the *News* continued as a daily publication, but did not attract as much circulation or advertising as the *Times*—except on Sunday, when it published the only paper. Larry and Kay Fanning bought the *News* in the 1960s for $450,000. Larry, who had newspaper experience in Chicago, died soon thereafter, and Kay continued operating the paper at a loss.

In 1974, Fanning entered into a joint operating agreement with the *Times*. The agreement allowed the editorial policies to remain distinct while production, circulation, and advertising operations were taken over by the *Times*. The deal enabled Atwood to take over the Sunday edition, which had represented a large percentage of the *News* income. The *News* countered by publishing an expanded Saturday paper, so Anchorage residents had the opportunity to take a "Sunday" paper with them on weekend trips. During this period, the *News* attracted a capable liberal staff and received a Pulitzer prize for investigating journalism. However, circulation of the morning paper continued to fail and, in February 1977, Fanning filed a $16.5 million lawsuit charging the *Times* with antitrust violations and breach of contract. The case was still in court when Fanning sold eighty percent of the *News* to the Sacramento-based McClatchy newspaper chain in 1979.

The McClatchy chain recognized the potential of the Anchorage newspaper market and subsidized the *News* as much as $10 million a year until the paper began to show an operating profit in 1985. In 1984 the daily circulation of the *News* reached 47,547, surpassing the *Times* by 4,000. Both papers published full Sunday editions, with the *News* circulation of 54, 918 being 10,000 more than the *Times*. The editorial policies of the two differed—the *News* being less concerned with economic development and more sensitive to environmental issues. The *News* generally favored Democratic candidates, while the *Times* supported Republicans. Anchorage residents who subscribed to both papers enjoyed the opportunity to read both sides of issues. Since advertisers and readers were willing to support both papers, they continued to operate profitably as long as the economic boom continued.

In the March 1985 *Alaska Business Monthly*, Editor Jerry Grilly of the *News* predicted, "It's possible that one day advertisers will be forced to choose one paper or the other. It's not going to happen in 1986 or 1987, but I think it will happen someday. We hope we can peacefully coexist with the *Times* forever; we just hope we can coexist a little better than they do."

The economic turnaround came sooner than Grilly predicted. In 1986 Arab oil producers flooded the world market with oil and the price of a barrel fell from $27 to $10. Between 1987 and 1989, Anchorage real estate lost up to half its value. Anchorage was overbuilt; 1,200 condominiums and homes were foreclosed, and strip malls stood vacant. In the summer of 1987, Anchorage 5th Avenue, Rainier Fund's $100-million downtown mall, opened, adding 230,000 square feet of unneeded retail space. Most of the 110 store spaces remained vacant for the rest of the decade. Oil companies cut production and falling state revenues brought an end to the dream of a Susitna Dam hydroelectric project. Waterborne cargo at the Port of Anchorage decreased thirty percent in 1986.

During the late 1980s recession, eight Anchorage banks closed. John Shively, the chief executive of United Bank Corporation, Alaska, Inc., wrote in 1987, "The majority of the people felt the real estate development boom would last forever...but Alaska banks were financing the building of condos, houses, and shopping centers. When the building stopped and other sectors of the economy began to disintegrate, people working in the construction industry and other ailing businesses began to leave and now we don't need all those condos, houses, and shopping centers." The Calista Native Corporation sold the Sheraton Hotel just before it would have declared bankruptcy. Other Native corporations suffered significant losses, but their lawyers softened the blow by devising a way to sell their losses to profitable corporations elsewhere in the United States. The economy was already so depressed in Alaska that the stock market crash on October 19, 1987 had little direct effect on the state.

Although the Alaska economy might have improved eventually on its own, it took another disaster to jump-start recovery. On March 27, 1989, the twenty-fifth anniversary of the 1964 earthquake, the *Exxon Valdez* oil tanker ran into Bligh Reef spilling 10.8 million gallons of North Slope crude oil into Prince William Sound. Anchorage escaped the direct devastation of the oil spill that several small coastal communities suffered. Both Anchorage and the impacted communities benefited from the influx of Exxon money during the cleanup effort that dominated Southcentral Alaska during the summer of 1989. About six percent of Anchorage households had at least one member working directly in the oil spill cleanup.

The largest beneficiary of the oil spill was probably VECO International, which specialized in oil industry support. When VECO's management learned of the oil spill, they immediately offered the company's services to Exxon. VECO renegotiated its contract with Exxon three times, earning $800 million in gross revenues. Not long after the *Exxon Valdez* disaster, VECO owner Bill Allen considered leaving Alaska for a less politically hostile part of the United States. Instead, he used some of his $32 million profit from the spill cleanup to buy the *Anchorage Daily Times* from the aging Bob Atwood. With the influx of VECO money, the newspaper war heated up as the decade of the nineties started. ∎

"Mister Tulsa," Tony Knowles

Tony Knowles earned his first title, "Mister Tulsa," as the first baby born in Tulsa, Oklahoma on January 1, 1943. In subsequent years he earned additional titles including borough assemblyman, municipal assemblyman, mayor of the Municipality of Anchorage, and governor of Alaska. Knowles graduated from Millbrook School in New York in 1959 and entered Yale University. His college education was interrupted by three years of military duty, which included a year in Vietnam with military intelligence. Upon return to the United States, he took courses at Columbia University while awaiting readmission to Yale, from which he graduated in 1968 with a degree in economics.

Immediately after graduation, Knowles married his wife, Susan, who graduated the same year from Vassar College. The following fall, the newlyweds left for Alaska, where Tony had a job with Loffland Brothers drilling company, which had drilled the North Slope discovery well in 1967. Knowles had worked summers in oil fields throughout the southwest while going to college. The couple settled in Anchorage while Tony worked a year in the North Slope and Cook Inlet oil fields before establishing his own business.

Knowles opened the Grizzly Burger, a fast-food hamburger restaurant, on the corner of Northern Light Boulevard and C Street in October 1969, several months before the first McDonald's started business on the next corner. In spite of competition, the business did well enough to justify starting additional Grizzly Burgers on Muldoon Road and in the University Center mall. The mall restaurant, renamed The Works, continued operation until 1990. In the summer of 1976, Knowles teamed with David and Fran Rose to open the Downtown Deli on Fourth Avenue.

Knowles was elected to the Greater Anchorage Area Borough Assembly in 1975 prior to unification and then won two more elections and served on the municipal assembly until 1979. He ran successfully for mayor in 1981 and again in 1984.

Although the economic collapse in Anchorage took place during Knowles' terms as mayor, he succeeded in completing the major building

Office of the Governor

Former Mayor Tony Knowles is the third Anchorage resident to be elected governor.

projects and enhanced recreational facilities in the municipality. In 1983 his administration established the Heritage Land Bank, a program that puts proceeds from the sale of surplus city lands into the Land Bank to be used for the purchase of other lands needed for municipal purposes. In a final settlement of the Municipal Land Entitlement Act in 1986 the State of Alaska conveyed 3,700 acres of land to the municipality. By 1988, the Land Bank had purchased $8.5 million worth of land for public purposes and had a balance of 13,000 acres in its account.

In addition to improvement and extension of fire control and police facilities, emergency health services, water and sewer, roads, and transit service, the Knowles administration opened the Brother Francis Shelter for the homeless in 1983 and Bean's Cafe in 1985. A five-year economic development strategy was devised, resulting in the 1987 creation of the Anchorage Economic Development Corporation, a public corporation dedicated to expanding and improving the Anchorage economy through specific projects.

After his two terms as Anchorage mayor, Knowles ran unsuccessfully for governor of Alaska in 1990 as a Democrat. In the 1994 election he was more successful, defeating the Republican candidate, James Campbell. During his first term as governor, Knowles had to deal with a state legislature dominated by conservative Republicans, resulting in frequent use of his veto power. While her husband was fighting competition from other restaurateurs and pursuing his political career, Susan Knowles served three six-year terms, from September 1975 to October 1993, as a Public Utilities Commissioner.

Knowles was elected to a second term as Governor of Alaska in 1998. He faces a challenge like the one he encountered as mayor of Anchorage in 1986 as the price of oil fell below $10 a barrel. ■

Office of the Governor

Governor Tony Knowles is no stranger to a hard hat. He worked on oil rigs in Cook Inlet and on the North Slope before entering the restaurant business.

King of the Strip Malls

Peter Zamarello, Anchorage's most flamboyant real estate developer during the expansive 1980s, built many of the one-story, strip malls that sprang up around town to house pizza parlors, convenience stores, and other small businesses. He was also the subject of the most dramatic rags-to-riches-and-back-to-rags local stories.

Zamarello was born in 1927 to poor Italian parents on the Mediterranean island of Cephalonia. Alaska was his goal when he left for America on a Greek freighter. His father, who had been in Anchorage during the construction of the Alaska Railroad in 1915, had frequently talked of the wonders and potential of the land. Soon after arriving in the United States, Zamarello obtained citizenship by marrying a Polish girl who was already a citizen.

Zamarello arrived in Anchorage in time to take part in the oil-leasing frenzy of the early 1960s and somehow got his hands on geological reports to help him bid on promising land. As soon as he made enough money for a down payment on a real estate loan, he built his first shopping center in Muldoon,

Elizabeth Tower

One of the strip malls built by the flamboyant real estate developer Peter Zamarello.

near the entrance to Elmendorf Air Force Base. When pipeline construction started in the 1970s, he opened an office in Beirut, Lebanon and sold Alaska land to wealthy Arabs. He soon joined the development frenzy, borrowing money, building, and borrowing more to create an empire of shopping centers, malls, office plazas, condos, and trailer parks. By 1985, Zamarello was the richest developer in the state. He constructed his malls wherever he chose because zoning in Anchorage was lax during the late 1970s and early 1980s.

When Tony Knowles became mayor in 1982, he reorganized the planning and zoning boards and revised the planning codes to protect wetlands and control strip zoning. Zamarello clashed with the new mayor over the city's refusal to issue him a permit to build a large hotel on land near International Airport that had been classified as wetlands. Although some developers slowed down in 1985 when economists warned of a building glut, Zamarello continued building. Even after the 1986 drop in oil prices compounded the problem, he disclosed plans for an eighteen-story bank building.

In August 1986, a contractor won a $4.2 million judgment against Zamarello and he filed for protection under Chapter 11 of the bankruptcy laws. Court examiners tried to unravel the intricacies of his seven interlocking companies and discover the whereabouts of his fortune. Some of the banks carrying Zamarello's uncollectible loans went broke or were forced into mergers. In an attempt to recoup losses, the Federal Deposit Insurance Corporation sued thirty-three former bank officers and directors for $55 million in 1991. Zamarello survived, but had to content himself with a much smaller office. To the regret of many Anchorage residents, the strip malls have also survived. ■

Pioneer Family Bankers

Two of the banks that survived the economic decline of the late 1980s are controlled by pioneer Anchorage families. Both the National Bank of Alaska, directed since 1919 by three generations of the Rasmuson family, and the First National Bank of Anchorage, acquired in 1943 by the Cuddy family, entered the 1990s in strong financial condition and have continued to expand.

Edward A. Rasmuson came to Yakutat, Alaska, in 1900 as a Swedish Covenant Missionary. While serving as a missionary, he studied law by correspondence and was admitted to the Alaska bar. In 1915 he was appointed U.S. Commissioner in Skagway and moved to that city with his family, which included his six-year-old son Elmer and nine-year-old daughter Evangeline. A year after arriving in Skagway, Rasmuson became corporate counsel for the Bank of Alaska, which had its main office in Skagway. He was elected president of the bank in 1919 and remained in that capacity until 1943, when he turned the reigns over to Elmer and became chairman of the board of directors.

Elmer Rasmuson grew up with the bank, serving as a janitor while going to school. After high school, he worked a year in the bank before going east to Harvard University, from which he graduated magna cum laude in 1930. While in college, Elmer worked summers in Anchorage and Ketchikan branches of the bank, and then spent a year operating the Cordova branch. He completed a master's degree at Harvard in 1933 and was working on a Ph.D. when he took accounting jobs in New York City with National Investors Corporation and Arthur Andersen and Company.

Edward Rasmuson asked his son to return to Alaska in 1943 because his health was failing. When Elmer took over management of the bank, the main office was still in Skagway, but since Anchorage was growing more than Skagway, Elmer moved the main office and his family to Anchorage in 1946. Elmer Rasmuson persuaded the first legislature after statehood to liberalize banking laws and permit locally owned banks to have outlying branches. In 1960 he engineered the merger of five other Alaskan banks—Miners and Merchant's Bank of Ketchikan, Bank of Wrangell, First Bank of Sitka, Bank of Homer, and Bank of Kodiak—with Bank of Alaska to form the National Bank of Alaska. The merger made NBA the largest bank in Alaska, with sixteen offices and total assets of about $60 million. Additional mergers with the Bank of Petersburg in 1972 and the Bank of Cordova in 1975 added to NBA's statewide coverage.

When Elmer Rasmuson was elected mayor of Anchorage shortly after the 1964 Good Friday earthquake, he turned the presidency of the bank over to Donald Mellish and became chairman of the board of directors. Rasmuson was mayor during the Alaska Purchase Centennial in 1967 when ground was broken for the Anchorage Museum of History and Art. Following his three-year term as mayor, he ran unsuccessfully for the United States Senate on the Republican ticket. Since then Rasmuson has served on various fisheries commissions and policy-making groups. His special expertise has been utilized in various public service roles, including president of the University of Alaska Board of Regents for thirteen years and first chairman of the Alaska Permanent Fund Corporation. In 1985 he was appointed to the Arctic Research Commission. Both Elmer and his wife, Mary Louise, a former colonel in the Women's Auxiliary Army Corps, have provided invaluable service as founders, patrons, and guiding lights for the Anchorage Museum of History and Art. As a board member of the Smithsonian's National Museum of Natural History, Rasmuson used his influence to bring the Arctic Studies Center to the Anchorage Museum. To celebrate his ninetieth birthday on February 15, 1999, Rasmuson announced the donation of $90 million to benefit Anchorage. Fifty million dollars were donated to the Anchorage Museum, and the Rasmuson Foundation received $40 million.

The National Bank of Alaska continues to be Rasmuson family

business. Elmer's son, Edward B. Rasmuson, assumed the bank presidency in 1975. Elmer has continued to hold various positions in the bank administration in addition to his public service activities.

Daniel Hon Cuddy spent his early childhood in Valdez, as did several other children destined to be Alaskan business and political leaders: Anchorage Mayor George Sullivan, Governor William A. Egan, and Permanent Fund Director John Kelsey. His father, Warren Cuddy, came to Valdez in the 1920s, serving as District Attorney in the Third Division Court before moving to Anchorage in 1932 to establish a private legal practice. In 1943 Warren Cuddy purchased a controlling interest in the First National Bank of Anchorage, which had opened in 1922.

Shortly before Warren Cuddy died suddenly in 1951, Dan had returned to Anchorage with a law degree after attending Stanford University and the University of Washington. As the only surviving son—his older brother David was killed in World War II—Dan had to choose whether to be a lawyer or a banker. He decided to set aside his legal career and assume the bank presidency, although he had no previous experience in banking. Throughout the growth of Anchorage, Cuddy has run a tight ship at the bank, which has grown to include over twenty branches throughout Alaska and more than a billion in assets. Although Dan Cuddy continues to be in charge at the bank, his oldest daughter, Betsy Lawer, has grown up in the bank and is assuming increasing responsibility. The Cuddy family continues to own over fifty percent of the bank stock. ■

Elizabeth Tower

Mayor George Sullivan used money from Alaska's new oil development to build the Performing Arts Building, part of the Project '80s construction boom.

11

A City Matures

Elizabeth Tower

Anchorage's downtown reflects the building boom of the 1980s.

Anchorage approached maturity in the 1990s. Slow, steady growth replaced the earlier boom-and-bust economy. An increasing population filled empty homes and offices built during the expansive eighties. Anchorage continues to be the urban center of Alaska's oil industry. Although production from Prudhoe Bay declined, improved recovery techniques allow for development of previously marginal fields. Tourism is replacing mining and fishing as Alaska's next most important industry, with Anchorage experiencing a new infusion of hotel space.

The population in Anchorage has changed; it is the largest "Native village" in Alaska. Immigrants are from Latin American, Korea, Russia, and Samoa rather than Scandinavia, the birthplace of many pioneer Anchorage residents. Older Alaskans retain residence in the state rather than moving to a warmer climate. Specialized professional services are available in Anchorage, which is the medical and legal referral center for the state and even the Russian Far East. Quality of life issues often take precedence over development for development's sake.

The *Exxon Valdez* oil spill confirmed environmentalists' concerns about the potential hazards of oil development in Alaska. Pictures of oil-soaked seabirds, seals, and sea otters filled newspapers throughout the world. Exxon mounted a monumental effort to clean the beaches of Prince William Sound and the Kenai Fiords National Park. Whether the cleanup efforts actually hastened the rehabilitation of the area is questionable, but the economic impact was considerable. The February 1990 issue of *Alaska Business Monthly* reported the "Exxon Air Force" was responsible for a sixty-percent boost in air freight passing through Anchorage International Airport.

Air cargo became the major activity at the Anchorage International Terminal. Most international passenger carriers stopped refueling in Anchorage when Russian air space opened up in the late 1980s. Use of Anchorage as a stop for passenger jets was further discouraged when a KLM jet suffered extensive damage after flying through a cloud of volcanic ash from the Mt. Redoubt eruption on December 15, 1989. By 1992 British Airways was the only airline offering a direct flight from Anchorage to Europe, and that flight stopped shortly thereafter. Despite Japanese investments in Alaska, such as SEIBU's new Alyeska Prince Hotel, even Japan Airlines stopped regular passenger service to Anchorage. KAL, Aeroflot, and China Airlines fly to Anchorage from Asia.

Refueling in Anchorage was still cost-effective for freight carriers because it enabled them to carry greater loads. In the early 1990s, Federal Express designated Anchorage International Airport as its distribution hub between Europe and Asia and built a large new headquarters facility. In July 1997 *Alaska Business Monthly* reported 82 cargo planes

Elizabeth Tower

A gondola at Alyeska takes visitors to the top of the mountain year-round.

were landing and departing from the airport each day and that 220 pilots and 465 ground crew were stationed in Anchorage.

Alaska Airlines started providing passenger flights between Anchorage and the Russian Far East to accommodate increased Russian presence in Alaska. As soon as the Cold War ended, Russian students started coming to Anchorage to attend the University of Alaska.

Anchorage adopted Magadan as a sister city, encouraging government officials and trade commissions to travel between the two cities. Russians traveling to Anchorage often purchase merchandise at local discount stores for resale at home.

Discount stores started moving into Anchorage in the late 1980s and continued throughout the 1990s. Price Savers and Costco were the first to enter the local market. WalMart, K-Mart, Eagle Hardware, Toys R Us, Borders, Barnes and Noble, and Home Depot have also opened stores, making it difficult for smaller local businesses to continue to make a profit. Small businesses, like MacKay's Hardware, have closed. Even the largest home-grown stores, such as Carr's Quality Food Centers, are being absorbed by national chains. After a game fight, the *Anchorage Daily Times* stopped publication in 1993, leaving the McClatchy-owned *Anchorage Daily News* as the only daily newspaper in town.

Alaska continues to be a popular summer tourist destination. Tours stop briefly in Anchorage enroute to Denali National Park, Katmai National Park, boat trips to watch marine wildlife, and other Alaskan destinations. But few cruise ships use the Anchorage port. Native groups hope to increase the appeal of Anchorage as a tourist destination by developing the Native Cultural Center on land donated by the Cook Inlet Regional Corporation. The Cultural Center, which opened in 1999, displays sample Eskimo, Indian, and Aleut villages. NANA, the Native corporation based in Kotzebue, is doing its share to assure that there is adequate hotel space in Anchorage to meet the anticipated demand. A joint venture with the Marriott hotel chain has resulted in construction of the 154-room Courtyard Suites for short-term visitors in addition to the Fairfield Suites and the Residence Inn for visitors planning longer stays. Marriott, in the meantime, is spending $40 million to build its own 20-story, 393-bed hotel. The Bristol Bay Native Corporation sold the Anchorage Westward Hilton to Hilton Hotel Corporation in 1997 in order to concentrate efforts on developing tourism in the Bristol Bay region. Cook Inlet Regional Corporation has also entered the tourism field with the purchase of Kenai Fjords Tours, which takes visitors from Seward to view marine animals in the Kenai Fjords National Park in seven vessels with 1,440 passenger capacity. CIRI also plans to develop a 200-space upscale RV park near the Native Cultural Center and is building a hotel with views of the McKinley range at Talkeetna, 100 miles north of Anchorage on the Alaska Railroad.

The Alaska Railroad, which celebrated its 75th Anniversary in 1998, has developed a profitable relationship with Princess Tours and Westours. Railroad assets, assessed at $22 million in 1985, when the state of Alaska purchased the railroad from the federal government, have increased to $130 million. The railroad earned a $10.7 million net profit in 1997. Federal investment continues to bolster the Anchorage economy, thanks partially to the efforts of Ted Stevens, Alaska's senior senator since 1968. In addition to highway and airport construction, major federal construction projects include the new Alaska Native Medi-

Elizabeth Tower

The Alaska Native Medical Center opened in 1996 replacing an older, now out-of-date facility. The new center offers medical service to the Native peoples throughout Alaska.

cal Center, opened in 1996, and a new hospital and post exchange at Elmendorf Air Force Base.

New hospital construction reinforces Anchorage's position as the medical center of Alaska. Hospitals, with over 20,000 employees, are among the largest industries in the state and Anchorage has more medical staff per capita than most American cities. Providence Hospital has increased its outreach to include management of satellite facilities at Seward and Kodiak. A succession of for-profit corporations assumed management of the hospital built by the Teamsters' Union in the 1970s. Currently operated by Columbia Hospital Corporation, Alaska Regional Hospital provides competition for Providence, but also teams with the larger hospital to avoid unnecessary duplication. All specialty services except for some forms of transplant surgery are available in Anchorage, which has over 500 physicians in private practice.

While growth in the medical profession has been considerable, it is surpassed by the influx of lawyers. The Alaska Native Settlement Claims Act (ANSCA), the Alaska Natural Interest Land Conservation Act (ANILCA), and the Exxon oil spill, in addition to the usual supply of murders, assaults, divorces, and civil suits, have resulted in enough litigation to keep over 1,000 Anchorage lawyers gainfully employed. Another professional field enjoying increased visibility, partially as a result of the oil spill, is environmental engineering. After realizing profit from the spill cleanup, VECO has joined other business in studying ways to protect the environment.

Although the majority of Alaskans would still favor opening the Arctic National Wildlife Refuge (ANWR) to oil exploration, the state has become more sensitive to environmental issues. Major challenges for the future include oil exploration in the National Petroleum Reserve, portions of which have recently been opened to exploration by the Interior Department, and construction of a natural gas pipeline from North Slope fields.

Environmental activists in Anchorage actively oppose extension of roads across park lands, and Mayor Rick Mystrom advertises the quality

of life in Anchorage by proclaiming it a "City of Lights and Flowers"—
lights in the winter and flowers in the summer. Many retired Alaskans,
convinced life in Anchorage is better than elsewhere in the United States,
have elected to stay in town rather than moving permanently to a warmer
climate. They are joined by retired military officers and oil executives
who discovered the city while assigned there. Anchorage may never
reach the national list of best retirement communities, but for people
who enjoy a change in seasons, natural beauty, and easy access to the
wilderness it has much to offer. An increasing number of three-genera-
tion families are living here. Anchorage population is approaching
300,000—which is remarkable considering that there were few, if any,
permanent residents in the area a hundred years ago. ∎

Elizabeth Tower

Murals decorate many buildings in downtown Anchorage.

Carrs—Alaska's Own Grocery Chain

Larry Carr came to Anchorage in 1947 because he heard construction jobs were available on Fort Richardson. He had just graduated from high school in Southern California, where jobs were scarce. Larry, who had worked in grocery stores back home, intended to return to California and start a store of his own, but prospects in Anchorage looked better. Working two jobs, he saved enough money to buy a Quonset hut market on Gambell Street. By 1952, Carr had

Anchorage Museum of History and Art

Larry Carr, who parlayed a quonset hut grocery store into a chain of supermarkets, worked to make his stores stand out from the competition with an emphasis on fresh produce.

replaced the Quonset with a building and brought his father, B.J. "Pop" Carr, up to help run the business. From the beginning Carr was an innovative retailer who believed in customer service. He even chartered a plane three times a week to bring fresh produce to Anchorage from the Lower 48.

In the early 1950s, Carr met Barney Gottstein, who had recently taken over a wholesale grocery business from his father. J.B. (Jake) Gottstein arrived in Anchorage in 1915, when it was a tent city, and set up business supplying miners and construction workers. The energetic Gottstein often used a dogsled team to carry a variety of wares to pioneers in the rugged Anchorage surroundings. On occasion he grubstaked the artist Sydney Laurence in exchange for paintings.

In Anchorage, Gottstein worked with Carr as a wholesaler, but they decided to collaborate in establishing a grocery store in Fairbanks. Barney was anxious to try his hand at the retail grocery but was reluctant to compete against his wholesale customers in Anchorage. Over the next thirty years the Carr-Gottstein partnership established stores throughout Alaska that were more than simply grocery stores. Carrs stores were quick to accept new merchandising opportunities: selling drugs, hardware, seasonal promotional goods, postage stamps, and theater tickets. They were the first West Coast stores to initiate salad bars. The twenty-four-hour urban stores are recognized as safe havens for people in trouble. In July 1998, a survey by Dittman Research Corp. found Carrs to be the most admired business in Alaska.

Although Carr specialized in retail and Gottstein in wholesale business, they worked together to develop the real estate, which included shopping centers, office buildings, industrial parks, and residential developments. In an interview with *Alaska Business Monthly*, Carr explained that "the combined strength made it possible to corner land and develop real estate." In the early 1950s Carr knew that Safeway was coming to town, so he set out to corner some of the better locations on long-term contracts while land prices were relatively low.

For almost fifty years the loyalty of Carr's customers enabled this homegrown grocery chain to survive challenges from the Safeway chain and, more recently, Fred Meyer stores. On August 7, 1998, Anchorage residents were shocked to hear that Safeway, Inc. was buying Carrs—including sixteen Carrs Quality Centers in Anchorage, Fairbanks, Palmer, Wasilla, Kenai, and Soldotna; nine Eagle Quality Centers in Seward, Homer, Valdez, and Unalaska; stores by other names in Nome, Kotzebue, Girdwood, Big Lake, and Seldovia; seventeen Oaken Keg liquor stores; and warehouse and wholesaling operations including a 233,000-square-foot facility in Anchorage—for $330 million.

Anchorage residents and 3,200 Carrs employees were stunned. Several economists at University of Alaska's Social and Economic Research Center protested that a monopoly would result from the combination of Alaska's two largest grocery retail chains. However, the subsequent announcement that Krogers is buying the Fred Meyer stores probably indicates that Anchorage will still have retail competition, though not with a homegrown business.

Larry Carr and Barney Gottstein must have been aware that the future was not bright for locally controlled business when they sold most of their interest in the company to top managers in 1990. They continue to support the Anchorage community through contributions to Alaska Pacific University which have enabled campus expansion. ■

Bringing Home the Bacon

Theodore Fulton Stevens was forty-five years old when Governor Walter J. Hickel appointed him to succeed Senator E.L. (Bob) Bartlett in December 1968. The appointment was unexpected but fortuitous for the young state. During his thirty-year career as Alaska's senior senator, Stevens has participated in negotiating all major legislation pertaining to Alaska and has succeeded beyond expectation in securing financial assistance from the federal government. Critics accuse Stevens of being one of the major promoters of congressional pork, but Alaskans, who appreciate the bacon he brings home, regularly reelect him in landslides.

Stevens was born in Indianapolis but was living in Chicago when the depression hit and his accountant father lost his job. His parents divorced when Ted was six years old, and the four Stevens children went back to Indiana to live with their grandparents. Subsequently his father developed severe eye problems and went blind. His three siblings went to California to live with their mother. Ted stayed behind to

Anchorage Museum of History and Art

Alaska Senator Ted Stevens greeted President and Mrs. Nixon when the First Couple visited Alaska in 1971

help his grandparents care for his father and a mentally retarded cousin. After his grandfather died, Ted moved to California, where he spent several happy years as a "beach bum" while he finished high school.

After graduating in 1942, Stevens enlisted in the Army Air Corps and was sent to Montana State University, where he scored so high on the aptitude test that he went immediately into flight training. After receiving his wings in early 1944, he was dispatched to China to fly for the 14th Army Air Corps Transport Section, which supported the Flying Tigers. For two years, Stevens piloted C-46 and C-47 cargo planes, often without escort, throughout the China theater to resupply Chinese units fighting the Japanese. By the time he left the Army Air Corps in March 1946, Stevens had collected a Distinguished Flying Cross for flying behind enemy lines, an Air Medal, and a Yun Hai Medal, awarded by the Chinese National Government.

The GI Bill enabled Stevens to graduate from UCLA in 1947 with a degree in political science and receive a law degree from Harvard University in 1950. Mike "Northcut" Ely, who had been Assistant Interior Secretary under President Herbert Hoover and then had started his own Washington D.C. office specializing in resource law, recruited Stevens directly from Harvard Law School. Stevens' first contact with Alaska came when Ely sent him to Fairbanks to help a client, Emil Usibelli, negotiate a contract to supply coal to the Army.

Stevens worked in General Dwight D. Eisenhower's successful presidential campaign. In anticipation of an appointment in the Interior Department, he resigned from Ely's law firm and married Ann Mary Cherrington, a Democrat who worked for the State Department during the Truman administration. When the Interior appointment did not materialize, Stevens accepted an offer to join Charles Clasby in his Fairbanks law firm and a $600 loan from Clasby to make the trip to Alaska. C.W. "Bill" Snedden, who had recently bought the *Fairbanks News-Miner*, and his wife, Helen, became close friends and mentors to the young couple. (Over thirty years later, when Snedden died in 1989, his bequest to Stevens of a yacht enabled Stevens to sell the boat for cash he needed to pay off debts.)

In September 1953, Stevens accepted a position as U.S. District Attorney in Fairbanks and earned a reputation as a tough prosecutor who carried a pistol on vice raids. Stevens lost his most noteworthy trial as a prosecutor to Anchorage lawyer Edgar Paul Boyko, who successfully defended a tax evader with the argument of "no taxation without representation," which resonated with a Fairbanks jury prior to statehood.

Stevens soon had his own opportunity to work behind the scenes for Alaska statehood. When Stevens went to Washington, D.C. in June 1954 as an assistant solicitor in the Interior Department, Eisenhower was opposed to statehood for Alaska because he thought it would be difficult to defend in case of invasion. However, when Fred Seaton replaced Douglas McKay as Interior Secretary, Alaska finally had a statehood advocate in the Eisenhower administration. Stevens worked closely with Seaton in drafting the Alaska statehood legislation and in preventing the partition of Alaska that Eisenhower had advocated. Stevens also helped the Alaska-Tennessee Plan delegation of William A. Egan, Ernest Gruening, and Ralph Rivers make appropriate contacts with Congressmen.

The long battle for statehood paid off when President Eisenhower signed the Alaska Statehood Bill on July 7, 1958. Three years later, in the last days of the Eisenhower administration, Stevens, as top lawyer in the Interior Department, wrote the public lands order creating the Arctic National Wildlife Refuge (ANWR). ANWR was created in an effort to end a much more sweeping land order that had withdrawn all of Arctic Alaska during World War II. As a result, Alaska was able to select the land where the Prudhoe Bay oil fields are now located.

After four years in Washington, D.C., Ann and Ted Stevens returned to Alaska with their five young children. Ted started a law practice in Anchorage in 1961, and promptly made his political debut by running unsuccessfully for the United States Senate as a Republican against incumbent Senator Ernest Gruening. Stevens was more successful in state elections, serving in the State House of Representatives from 1964-68 and as house majority leader in 1967 and 1968. Elmer Rasmuson beat Stevens in the

1968 Republican primary election for U.S. Senate and then lost to Mike Gravel in the general election.

While Stevens was in the state legislature, Governor Wally Hickel and the Republican-controlled legislature, realizing that both Senator Gruening and Senator Bartlett might die while in office, succeeded in passing legislation that would allow the governor to appoint a successor that was not of the same political party as the senator who died. Hickel was still governor in December 1968 when Senator Bartlett died. Hickel was about to become Interior Secretary in the Nixon administration, when he appointed Stevens to succeed Bartlett, realizing the benefit of having an aggressive young Republican senator with firsthand knowledge of Washington, D.C. and the Interior Department. Since the Stevens appointment preceded the beginning of Mike Gravel's first term in the Senate, Stevens became Alaska's senior senator.

Stevens and Gravel worked together on the 1971 Alaska Native Claims Settlement Act. Stevens answered critics who didn't want Natives to receive any land by arguing that any means of getting federal land into private ownership would benefit the state. He also supported cash settlement for the Natives as a means for stimulating the economy. Stevens and Gravel tangled during negotiations on the Alaska National Interest Lands Conservation Act (ANILCA), when Gravel blocked acceptance of a compromise bill that Stevens believed would be the best deal available for Alaska. The final bill, passed in 1980 during the Carter administration, resulted in more land being placed in reservations than would have been the case had Gravel not blocked the first compromise bill. The delay in passage of the Alaska lands bill was especially bitter for Stevens.

The Learjet in which he was returning from Governor Hammond's inauguration in Juneau to attend land hearings in Anchorage crashed at Anchorage International Airport on December 8, 1978. Stevens was one of two survivors; his wife, Ann, died in the crash.

Two years later, he married Catherine Bittner Chandler and became the father of another daughter at age fifty-seven.

Although Stevens has participated in all the landmark Alaska legislation during his thirty years in Congress, he will probably be remembered for his success in feeding the Alaskan economy with federal money. He protected Alaskan military bases, brought the 6th Light Infantry Division to Alaska, and promoted facilities like the Elmendorf Air Force base hospital. He helped Native corporations escape bankruptcy by sponsoring legislation that allowed them to sell their losses to profitable corporations seeking tax shelters from 1986 to 1988 when the Alaskan economy crashed. Anchorage's most visible evidence of Stevens' largesse is the new $150-million Alaska Native Medical Center, which opened in 1996.

Senator Stevens is still bringing home the bacon. When the 105th Congress convened on January 7, 1997, Stevens assumed the chairmanship of the Senate Appropriations Committee. In this position he is at the peak of his ability to deliver money to the state that he helped shape over forty years ago as a young Interior Department lawyer. The 1998 budget allocated about half a billion federal dollars for projects in Alaska, among which are several for Anchorage, including $28 million for an elevated Alaska Railroad terminal at the Anchorage International Airport. ■

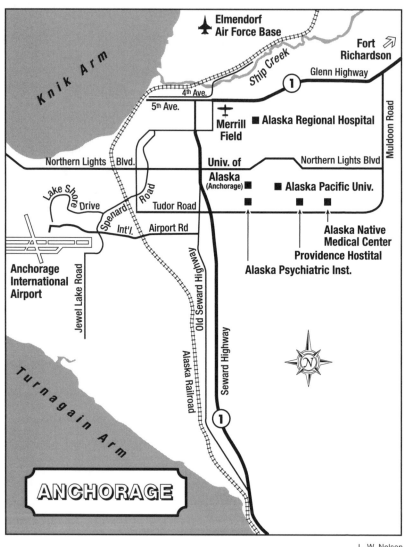

L. W. Nelson

Bibliography

General

Alaska Geographic Society, Vol. 23, No. 1, 1996. *Anchorage*.

———, Vol. 5, No. 1, 1977. *Cook Inlet Country*.

Atwood, Evangeline. *Anchorage, All American City*. Portland, Oregon: Binford and Mort, 1957.

———, *Anchorage, Star of the North*. Tulsa, Oklahoma: Continental Heritage Press, 1982.

Carberry, Michael, and Donna Lane. *Patterns of the Past, An Inventory of Anchorage's Historical Resources*. Municipality of Anchorage Community Planning Dept., 1986.

Carlson, Phyllis, Mike Kennedy, and Cliff Cernick. Anchorage: *The Way It Was*. Municipality of Anchorage Historic Landmark Commission, 1981.

Fond Memories of Anchorage Pioneers, Part 1—Personal Histories Written by Pioneers of Alaska, Igloo 15, Auxilliary 4. Anchorage, 1996.

Haycox, Stephen. *A Warm Past*. Anchorage: Press North, 1988.

Rakestraw, Lawrence W. A. *History of the United States Forest Service in Alaska*. Anchorage: Alaska Historical Society, 1981.

Richards, Robert R. *Alaska Business and Industry*. Anchorage: Windsor Publications Inc., 1989.

Wilson, William H. *Railroad in the Clouds. The Alaska Railroad in the Age of Steam, 1914-1945*. Boulder, Colo.: Pruett Publishing Co., 1977.

Arrival of White Settlers

Barry, Mary. *Seward Alaska, Part I: Prehistory to 1914*. Anchorage: M.J.B.

Buzzell, Rolfe G. (ed.) *Memories of Old Sunrise, Gold Mining on Alaska's Turnagain Arm*. Anchorage: Cook Inlet Historical Society, 1994.

DeArmond, R.N. "And So It Was Named Girdwood" in *Alaska Sportsman*, June, 1962.

Girdwood Historical Times, Vol. 1. Girdwood: Alyeska Chronicle, 1981.

Glenn, Edward F. *Cook Inlet Exploring Expedition in Alaska 1899. Narratives of Exploring in Alaska*. Washington, D.C., 1900.

Sherwood, Morgan. *Explorations in Alaska, 1865-1900*. Fairbanks: University of Alaska Press, 1992.

Tower, Elizabeth. *Mining, Media, Movies: Cap Lathrop's Keys to Alaska's Riches*. Anchorage, 1990.

Alex, Dan. Interview, April 8, 1998.

Chandonnet, Ann. *The Once and Future Village of Ikluat/Eklutna*. Chicago: Adams Press, 1979.

——— . *On the Trail of Eklutna*. Anchorage: User Friendly Press, 1979.

——— . "Icons and Obedience: Mike Alex," *The Great Lander*, Vol. 8, No.16, 1976.

Kari, James and James A. Fall. *Shem Pete's Alaska*. University of Alaska Native Language Center, 1987.

Stephan, Alberta. "Athabaskans of Upper Cook Inlet" in *Adventures Through Time*.

Yarborough, Michael R. "A Village Which Sprang Up Before My Very Eyes, An Historical Account of the Founding of Eklutna" in Davis, William and Nancy. *Adventures Through Time*. Anchorage: Cook Inlet Historical Society, 1996.

Townsite Auction and Railroad Town

Anchorage Daily Times. 11/28/16; 11/18-23/16; 12/18/16; 1/4/17; 4/17/17; 10/5/18; 8/20/19.

Cook Inlet Pioneer. 8/14/15; 8/21/15; 6/5/15; 7/17/15.

Cordova Daily Times. 6/29/15.

Gideon, Kenneth. *Wandering Boy, Alaska 1913 to 1918*. Fairfax, Virginia: East Publishing Company, 1967.

The Seward Gateway. 11/29/16; 12/15/16; 12/18/16.

"Joe Spenard" in *Anchorage: The Way It Was*.

End of the Boom

Stolt, William and Lilian. *Bill and Lily, Two Alaskans*. Anchorage: Publication Consultants, 1997.

Tower, Elizabeth. *Mining, Media, Movies, Cap Lathrop's Keys to Alaska's Riches*. Anchorage, 1990.

Woodward, Kesler E. *Sydney Laurence, Painter of the North*. Seattle: University of Washington Press, 1990.

"Leopold David" in *A Warm Past*.

"Leopold David" in *Patterns of the Past*.

Anchorage Daily Times, 11/22/24.

Depression Farmers Come North

Atwood, Evangeline. *We Shall Be Remembered*. Anchorage: Alaska Methodist University Press, 1966.

Hawley, Charles, Unpublished manuscript on Wesley Earl Dunkle.

Irwin, Don. *The Colorful Matanuska Valley*. Anchorage, 1968.

Miller, Orlando. *The Frontier in Alaska and the Matanuska Colony*. New Haven: Yale University Press, 1975.

Stoll, William M. *Hunting for Gold in Alaska's Talkeetna Mountains, 1897-1951*. Greensburg, Pa.: Chas. M. Henry Printing Co., 1997.

Satterfield, Archie. *The Alaska Airline Story*. Anchorage: Northwest Publishing Co., 1981.

Tefford, Bill. "Recollections of Early Day Transportation Systems in Alaska," Letter to Governor William A. Egan, 1968.

"Otto Ohlson and His Era" in *Railroad in the Clouds*.

"Czar Otto Ohlson" in *A Warm Past*.

"Depressing '30s; 1928-40" in *Anchorage, All American City*.

War Effort Energizes City

Chandonnet, Fern (ed.). *Alaska at War: Papers for the Alaska at War Symposium*. Anchorage, November 11-13, 1995.

Cochran, Marjorie. *Between Two Rivers: The Growth of Chugiak-Eagle River*. Alaska Historical Commission Studies in History, No. 26, 1982.

Cohen, Stan. *The Forgotten War, A Pictorial History of World War II in Alaska and Northwestern Canada*. Missoula, Mont.: Pictorial History Publishing Co., 1981.

Cole, Terence. "Boom Town Anchorage and the Second World War" in Schwantes, Carlos (ed.). *The Pacific Northwest in World War II*.

Garfield, Brian. *The Thousand Mile War*. New York: Ballantine Books, 1971.

Gruening, Ernest. *Many Battles: The Autobiography of Ernest Gruening*. New York: Liveright, 1973.

Klouda, Warren and Naomi. "Homesteaders" in *Anchorage Magazine*, Vol. 1, No. 1, Sept.-Oct., 1989.

O'Malley, Barbara. Interview, August 1998.

Potter, Jean. *Alaska Under Arms*. New York: The MacMillan Co., 1942.

———. "Robert Reeve" in *The Flying North*. New York: Ballantine Books, 1972.

Salisbury, C.A. *Soldiers of the Mist*. Missoula, Mont.: Pictorial Histories Publishing Co. 1992.

Tower, Elizabeth. "Japanese Sourdoughs." Unpublished manuscript.

Sand Lake Elementary School 6th Grade Students. *History of the Sand Lake Area*.

O'Malley Elementary School 6th Grade Students. *The Homesteaders: The Hillside, a History*.

"Homesteading" in *Patterns of the Past*.

"General Simon Bolivar Buckner, an Army Hunter in Alaska" in *A Warm Past*.

"Reeve Aleutian Airways" in *Alaska Business and Industry*.

The Battle for Statehood

Campbell, L.J. "August G. Hiebert" in *Alaska Business Monthly*, January 1989.

Chlupach, Robin. *Airwaves Over Alaska: The Story of Pioneer Broadcaster Augie Hiebert*. Issaquah, Wa.: Sammamish Press, 1992.

"Northern Television, Inc." in *Alaska Business and Industry*.

Kolb, Richard K. "Alaska, Cold War's Strategic Frontier, 1945-1991" in *VFW*, April, 1998.

Reynolds, Georgeanne Lewis, *Historical Overview and Inventory: White Alice Communications System*. Prepared for USAF Alaska Air Command, April 1988.

The Coldest Front: Cold War Military Properties in Alaska (draft). United States Department of Defense Legacy Resource Management Program. Prepared in Cooperation with the Alaska State Historic Preservation Office, February 1996.

Site Summit, Nike Hercules Missile Installation. Alaska Office of History and Archeology, June 1996.

"Anchorage Times" in *Alaska Business and Industry*.

"Interview With Robert Atwood" in *Anchorage Magazine*, May 1990.

"David and Goliath" and "Robert B. Atwood" in *Alaska Business Monthly*, March 1985.

"Robert B. Atwood" in *Alaska Business Monthly*, January 1988.

"Atwood Dead at Age 89." *Anchorage Daily News*, 1/11/97.

"Civic Leader Evangeline Atwood Dies." *Anchorage Daily Times*, 11/6/87.

"Irene Ryan." *Anchorage Daily News*, 11/26-27/97.

"Mt. Spurr Eruption." *Anchorage Daily Times*, 7/9-14/53.

The Good Friday Earthquake

"Alaska Pacific University" in *Alaska Business and Industry*.

Committee on the Alaska Earthquake of the Division of Earth Sciences Natural Research Council. *The Great Alaska Earthquake of 1964*, Human Ecology. Washington, D.C.: National Academy of Sciences, 1970.

Laird, Paul. "Walter J. Hickel" in *Alaska Business Monthly*, January 1988.

———. "Hickel Investment Company" in *Alaska Business Monthly*, November 1985.

Hickel, Walter J. *Who Owns America?* New York: Paperback Library, 1971.

Roberts, Malcolm B. *The Wit and Wisdom of Wally Hickel*. Anchorage: Searchers Press, 1994.

Roderick, Jack. *Crude Dreams, A Personal History of Oil and Politics in Alaska*. Fairbanks/Seattle: Epicenter Press, 1997.

Sewell, Sammye Taplin. Interview, October 1998.

Strohmeyer, John. *Extreme Conditions; Big Oil and the Transformation of Alaska*. Anchorage: Cascade Press, 1997.

Tower, Elizabeth. *Umbrella Guide to Skiing in Alaska*. Fairbanks/Seattle: Epicenter Press, 1997.

The Oil Boom Years

Cole, Dermot. *Amazing Pipeline Stories: How Building the Trans-Alaska Pipeline Transformed Life in America's Last Frontier*. Fairbanks/Seattle: Epicenter Press, 1997.

Hammond, Jay. *Tales of Alaska's Bush Rat Governor*. Fairbanks/Seattle: Epicenter Press, 1994.

Hanrahan, John and Peter Gruenstein. *Lost Frontier*. New York: W.W. Horton, 1977.

Hipshman, Laurence E. *Spenard: The Development of an Anchorage Community*. A Paper Presented at Alaska Historical Society Annual Meeting, October 21, 1997.

"Hijacking of Wien Jet" in *Anchorage Daily Times* 10/18-19/71; *Anchorage Daily News* 10/19-20/71.

Hollunbuck, Nancy Davis. Interview, August 1998.

Hood, Mary H. *A Fan's Guide to the Iditarod*. Loveland, Co.: Alpine Blue Ribbon Books, 1996.

McGinnis, Joe. *Going to Extremes*. New York: Alfred A. Knopf, 1980.

McPhee, John. *Coming Into the Country*. New York: Farrar, Straus and Giroux, 1976.

Sherwonit, Bill. *Iditarod: The Great Race to Nome.* Anchorage/Seattle: Alaska Northwest Books, 1991.

"Alaska's Business Pioneers: George M. Sullivan" in *Alaska Business*, March 1984.

"Profile: George Sullivan, a Retrospect of Anchorage's Potent Mayor" in *Alaska Industry*, July 1981.

The Decade of Prosperity

Alaska Business Monthly, January 1982 - December 1989.

"Cook Inlet Region, Inc." in *Alaska Business and Industry*.

Dixon, Robert F. "Pete Zamarello" in *Alaska Business Monthly*, April 1984.

"Elmer Rasmuson - Interview" in *Alaska Business Monthly*, January 1984.

"Elmer Rasmuson: Piloting Growth of Alaska's Financial Industry" in *Alaska Business Monthly*, December 1982.

Fuerst, Judith. "Elmer E. Rasmuson" in *Alaska Business Monthly*, March 1887.

Knowles, Susan. Interview, September 1998.

Laird, Paul. "Cuddy's Three C's of Banking: Conservative, Consistant, Cash on Hand" in *Alaska Business Monthly*, January 1985.

Scagliotto, Lisa. "D.H. Cuddy" in *Alaska Business Monthly*, January 1993.

A City Matures

Alaska Business Monthly, January 1990 - September 1998.

Anchorage Indicators - 1996. Anchorage: Municipality of Anchorage Department of Community Planning and Development, 1996.

"Bernard J. Gottstein" in *Alaska Business Monthly*, January 1989.

"Carr-Gottstein Inc." in *Alaska Business and Industry*.

"Dropping Anchor: City begins to grow roots" in *Anchorage Daily News*, 10/4/98.

"Larry J. Carr" in *Alaska Business Monthly*, January 1988.

"Safeway Buys Carrs" in *Anchorage Daily News*, 8/7/98.

"Senior Senator: Big Voice for Alaska" in *Anchorage Daily News*, 8/7-13/94.

"Spoils of Battle: Tenacious Stevens secures millions," *Anchorage Daily News*, 10/24/98.

Index

220